Remembering Vietnam
50 Years Later

From Colfax to Con Thien.

William G. Ward

ISBN: 978-1517090678

ISBN-10 1517090679

Bill Ward

Acknowledgements

A very grateful acknowledgement to **Hal Taylor**, who has spent a large portion of his own personal time with the background research and general editing of this book. When I first mentioned that I was going to write about my time in military service, he generously offered his help. We both knew that the hardest part of writing a book may be the writing itself, but, by far, the most labor intensive, time consuming, and painstaking part is the editing process, which can sometimes take twice as long to complete.

Hal has been tireless in supplying me with reams of notes on necessary corrections, suggested corrections, and ideas where I might expand on the material I have written about. From the very beginning, Hal has let me be the one to decide whether I include them or not. In almost all cases, I have incorporated his suggestions and corrections. However, I may have not always been as meticulous about making sure that the editorial updating made its way to the final document. In those instances, and I hope they are few; the fault lies with the author, and not the editor.

Hal and I have known each other since our earliest school days, and we both accept that there has always been a difference in our methodologies. His has always been, "If something is worth doing, it is worth doing right." and mine has always been, "It's close enough!"

I can only admire the sheer courage it took for him to let me be the final, editorial arbiter for this book.

Thank You Hal!

Table of Contents

DEDICATION

To my wife Jeanne; my two daughters, Alicia and Jessica; and my grandchildren.

To the memory of my brother, Bob, who also served in Vietnam, and to the memory of our beloved, younger brother, Jim, who became a fireman and paramedic, and served his community and his country for his entire life.

Finally, to the memory of my fallen comrades who did not return from Vietnam, and most especially, to the memory of Lt. John Peter Manzi, who was KIA on September 7, 1967. He died heroically at the battle of "The Churchyard," near Hill 48, just southwest of Con Thien,[1] a firebase near the DMZ. And finally, to the memory of Sgt. Calvin Rhett Holley, who was my squad leader in Vietnam, and later, my great friend and mentor during the last years of his life.[2]

Taking a break while on patrol: Sgt. Holley and Lt. Manzi

---

[1] Con Thien means the "Hill of Angels" in Vietnamese.

[2] Sgt. Holley wrote his own book of memoirs of his time as a Marine: *Memories of an Old Marine*. Publisher: Boggy Bottom Publishing Company.

FOREWORD

The idea of writing about my time in the Marine Corps came to me a few years ago. I was watching a PBS special about WWII. The subject was a pilot in the Army Air Corps, a young Lieutenant, flying a P-47 over Nazi-controlled Belgium. He was shot down and forced to make a landing. Fortunately, he was found by members of the Belgium Resistance, who came to his aid.

Shortly into the television program, I began to realize that this man, the young pilot, was my own uncle, Lt. Bill Grosvenor. He spent seven months moving from safe house to safe house as he tried to make his way back to England. Eventually, he was captured by the Nazis, and put into prison, where he remained until liberated by advancing Allied forces.

Not only had I been unaware of most of my uncle's WWII experiences, I knew virtually nothing about my own father's time in the service. From casual remarks my father had made when I was about 11 or 12, I did know that he had been in the Army during WWII. He had mentioned that he had served in the Pacific (on the island of Okinawa), but other than that, I knew almost nothing.

My mother and father didn't meet until after WWII, so I had no records or letters to go from. I did write to the Department of the Army, requesting his military records using an official SF-180 form, but after waiting nearly nine months, I received a letter back saying that "Unfortunately, your father's records had been destroyed in the 1973 Kansas City fire at the National Personnel Records Center."[3]

To add to the difficulties of telling my own story was the fact that many of my memories of that time, from some 48 years ago, were patchy at best. When I returned from Vietnam, I was sent to a new duty station and would not see or talk to anyone from my old unit again for many years.

---

[3] *See* Chapter Notes

I had worked very hard at trying to put most of those Vietnam memories behind me. As I came to find out, that rarely works very well. The memories just get pushed deeper into your subconscious, making them more difficult to recall, but with a nasty habit of percolating back to the surface during stressful times, sometimes many years later.

But then things took a fortunate turn. My wife was digging through a box of old papers and memorabilia in our garage, and came across a large packet of old letters. They were addressed to my Mom and had been sent by me while I was overseas. Years later, they were found and saved by my brother, Jim, who then passed them on to me.

In all, there were nearly 70 letters, and they had been sent while I was in Vietnam. It was like a miracle finding them again, because I had searched for a long time, and was sure that they were lost.

As I carefully read through each one, it amazed me how the memories came back. All the letters were dated, and I almost always included the places and activities that I was engaged in. I never included anything that I felt might upset my Mom, because that would have served no purpose. I did include such things as when I was promoted, when my duties changed from being a rifleman to a radio operator, and general descriptions of the land and terrain and the weather. I found that the dates alone were a tremendous help in making sense of my own fragmented memories.

Probably the single biggest windfall (actually a blessing) was when I got back in contact with Rhett Holley, my old squad leader from Vietnam. It's difficult, if not impossible, to really talk about some of those experiences unless you're talking to someone who also lived through them. Rhett was the first person I met when I arrived in Vietnam (I was a new replacement, assigned to his squad), and he was the last person I said goodbye to when I left.

After Vietnam, Rhett and I (and several others from our platoon) had been shipped directly to Okinawa to go through medical processing and recuperation before being reassigned to other duties. Rhett's 13-

month combat tour had been completed, so he was sent back to the States. I, however, still had five months left of my original 13-month tour. So, after my recuperation in Okinawa, I was sent to Camp Smith, Hawaii to finish out my time.

Because we had both been awarded three Purple Hearts[4], Rhett and I would not be allowed back into a combat area unless we filed a series of waivers, or re-enlisted in the Marine Corps. Effectively, our combat careers were over, and we would both be reassigned to non-combat duties, which is what happened.

Reconnecting with Rhett after 48 years, I had a hundred questions for him: "Whatever happened to this person? When did this or that happen?" Sometimes I would remember certain events differently, or from a different viewpoint, and just being able to talk to someone who was there, and who had experienced it as well, was a great help in putting my thoughts into perspective.

One thing that did shock me was to discover that I wasn't the only one who was having trouble recalling events. As I got more contact information, and had an opportunity to communicate with some of my old buddies from Vietnam, I found out that many still suffered from the effects of concussion wounds, and in some cases, traumatic memory loss.

Back during the Vietnam era, when someone was discharged back to civilian life, they were pretty much left on their own to deal with the lingering emotional scars that were still there. Some scars would never heal completely. It would be another 20-30 years before we would even hear the term "PTSD." let alone realize that most of us would come to look upon these troubling "personal issues" as a weakness that we had to hide from everyone else. There was a period of time in the 1980s that I took to answering "No" to the question, "Were you ever in the military?" simply to avoid the subject altogether.

---

[4] The rule of "Three Purple Hearts and you're pulled from combat" was first enacted during the Korean War, and then was carried through the Vietnam War as well.

One of the most common problems that veterans experience when there has been a tremendous amount of personal loss is a sense of guilt. Nowadays, it is called, "survivor's guilt." When so many of your comrades have been killed, or have lost arms and legs, or been blinded, you begin to ask yourself, "Why did I come through it?" There really are no good answers to that question, other than sheer luck.

Rhett sent me a copy of a book that had been written in in the late 1980s entitled, *Ambush Valley – The Story of a Marine Infantry Battalion's Battle for Survival*. It was written by Eric Hammel, who is an author of military history books. The book is about the last, pivotal battle that Rhett and I fought with our unit near Con Thien, a firebase near the DMZ. The entire book is just about those four days in September of 1967, when my unit (the 3/26th)[5] was engaged in a life-or-death struggle with an entire NVA[6] regiment about three miles southwest of the Con Thien.

Hammel took a unique approach when writing his book; he contacted and interviewed many of the officers and NCOs[7] who participated in that battle. Through use of direct statements and quotes, he was able to give a fairly accurate, and often very personal, accounting of what transpired. I say "fairly accurate," because, while the book does do a good job with the timeline of events, and provides snatches here and there that reflect the immediate experiences of the individuals being quoted, in actual practice, no one individual, book or movie can ever hope to capture the enormity of what transpired during those four days. In the 3rd Battalion's archives, it is noted as being the deadliest month in its entire history, even more so than when the 3/26th landed on the beaches of Iwo Jima in WWII.

---

[5] 3rd Battalion, 26th Marine Regiment, 5th Marine Division. In mid-March of 1967, the 5th Marine Division command was turned over to the 3rd Marine Division.

[6] North Vietnamese Army

[7] NCO – is a non-commissioned officer, i.e., an enlisted man of rank Corporal (E-4) or higher.

But my story is not just about that last battle. I wanted this story to be about the day-to-day experiences, as I remember them, what it was like, from my own perspective, to go through the days of monsoon rains, the intense heat of tropical jungles, about meeting the peasant farmers who lived in the countryside, and the Montagnard "Mountain People" of the Central Highlands, and the beautiful landscapes that made the experience so surreal.

I even wanted to recount some of the more memorable times, like when our night patrol encountered a tiger, and when I came face-to-face with an Asian cobra. I wanted to describe what it was like when we bivouacked one night in the courtyard of a King's mausoleum (with a giant chessboard in the entry way), and when we would take Montagnard scouts on our patrols, and the time one of our guys shot the helmet off my head when he was cleaning his pistol. I also wanted to tell about some of the mistakes I made, and how I learned from those mistakes.

And finally, I want to tell my children and grandchildren about the men that I served with. Some were just like me, a young Marine who simply wanted to do his duty. Some were extraordinary people, like my platoon commander, Lieutenant John Manzi, and my squad leader, Rhett Holley. They were true heroes and an inspiration to us all. Without them, I probably would not have made it back home to write this book.

Chapter 1

Colfax

I was born in Colfax, Iowa, a small, farming community in central Iowa with a population of around 2300. I was raised in an average-sized family (for those times) of 3 brothers and 1 sister and an older half-brother and sister from my dad's first marriage.

I had always thought of Colfax as being a large city, and I guess it was by Iowa standards. Once, when I was about 15 years old, I came across an Iowa road map and I noticed that on the back side there was a list of all the towns in Iowa, listed alphabetically. Next to each town's name was the 1960 census population for that town. I also noticed that there were exactly 1000 towns in total. This intrigued me. It was summer vacation, so with nothing better to do, I spent the next two days re-writing the list. This time I listed them all by population. It wasn't an easy task. I finally decided that the easiest way to accomplish this was to get 10 sheets of paper and write the name of each town in its own corresponding block of 1-100, 101-200, 201-300, etc. Things went much faster after that.

Once I was completely done I was able to review my handiwork and make some conclusions, and many surprised me. The very first thing I noticed was that, yes, Colfax was indeed a large town, it was larger than 83% of the cities and towns in Iowa. I also learned that the median-population of Iowa towns was about 500, and that the bottom 50% of all Iowa towns had populations of 300 or less.

To my young, naive mind, this was all I needed to confirm my original suspicions that "Colfax was indeed a large city". And although we did have a few *even larger* cities in the state of Iowa, they were the exceptions rather than the rule.

And why shouldn't Colfax be considered a large city? We already had everything that a big city was supposed to have. We had a large manufacturing business (the Monroe Table Company), we had a public library, a school (kindergarten through high school), a town newspaper, and a large business district that boasted a bank, two grocery stores, two drug stores, and a city park. We even had a movie theater at one time, but it was later replaced by a bowling alley.

I can remember, when I was 11 or 12 years old, my favorite day was always a Saturday. Typically, my brothers and I, after collecting our allowances of $.25 each, would head out the door looking for adventure. The first stop was the Colfax library, where our grandmother worked as the city librarian. She would sometimes give us her loose change or she might have some candy or cookies that she'd brought with her.

Next we'd stroll downtown, looking through the store front windows. I particularly liked going into the jewelry and sporting goods store owned by Royal Cross. Sometimes there would be BB-guns on display, and other times there were some neat toys that we could dream about for our birthdays or Christmas. Then it was across the street to Weirick's Drug Store to shop for a candy bar (the big Babe Ruth bars only cost 10 cents), then next down to Taylor's Drug Store, where they made the best "Green Rivers" you ever tasted. We'd stay awhile, loitering by the comic book rack, pretending to be just browsing, but all the while, reading through them as fast as we could before we got shooed out.

We'd keep walking all the way down to the Sale Barn area[8], where we'd sneak back into the hay barns and make tunnels and forts and play war games. We could usually get away with this for several hours until old Pete Briles would spot us and run us out. We always thought he was just being mean, but in retrospect, I realize that it was a dangerous place to be playing. Still, sometimes, when we'd

---

[8] Where farmers sold livestock on Saturdays.

look back, we'd see him smiling or laughing, probably remembering the days when he was our age and used to do the very same thing.

I guess my point is that growing up in Colfax was an idyllic time for most of the kids of my generation. Our impressions of the outside world came from television, or the movies, and things like wars and fighting were something that we thought had never touched our town. We learned about those kinds of things in history books.

When we were kids, we would sometimes divide up into teams and "play war," although it was more like a big game of "hide-and-seek." than anything else. I once asked my dad if he'd ever been in the Army, and he just smiled and made some kind of joke about, "being an instructor for the Japanese." My mother heard him say that and scolded him, "Now, Reed Ward, don't get Billy all confused."

Many years would pass before I came to learn that the small town that I lived in had been deeply affected by war. When I used to deliver newspapers, around age 11 and 12, I can remember seeing Blue Star banners (and, sadly, sometimes a Gold Star[9]) adorning a window, but not knowing what they meant.

My grandmother, the town librarian, had four sons in WWII, three had been with units like the 82nd Airborne that fought in Europe, and one son was the young P-47 pilot that I spoke about earlier.

Royal Cross, the jeweler, had been in the Army, and had been awarded the Bronze Star. Mr. George Weirick had been a Naval Officer; Mr. Harold Taylor had been a United States Marine; Norman Earl Ellsworth, the uncle of Robert Van Elsen and a member of my Mom's graduating class, died heroically aboard the USS Whitehurst in the waters around Okinawa, fighting off Japanese dive bombers; and Mr. Briles, the quiet farmer who used to chase us

---

[9] These banners first became a way, during WWI and WWII, for households to indicate they had family members in the service. If the star was "Gold", it meant that a serviceman had been killed in the war.

out of the hay barns in the summer, had been a tank commander and was awarded the Congressional Medal of Honor. He not only saved the lives of several soldiers by pulling them out of a burning tank, he had also, single-handedly, captured 50 German prisoners.

And my dad, who had once joked with me about his service, had been part of the landing force that took over the occupation of some of the Pacific Islands like Okinawa. Prior to leaving for the Pacific, he had been an Army rifle instructor for one of the Nisei (Japanese-American) battalions training in California. That battalion would become one of the most highly decorated units of WWII[10].

I eventually came to realize that almost every single family in my hometown had, in some way, served or sacrificed for their country during WWII. But no one ever talked about it. Instead they talked about 4-H fairs, church barbeques, and our girls' basketball team. Those were the things that were most important to them. When their Country called them, they had stepped up and served with great distinction, and then quietly returned home and got on with their lives. I can see now why they were called "Our Greatest Generation."

WWII Blue Star Flag

---

[10] *See* references in Chapters Notes (Chapter 1 – "Colfax").

Chapter 2

The Spring and Summer of 1966

It was a Friday morning, and I was sitting in my third-period study hall, thinking about what I was going to do for the summer. It was the last week of May, my senior year, and there was only about a week left in school, and then - hooray! - I'd be graduating.

Unlike a lot of my classmates, I really didn't see myself going off to college right away. I could have, I suppose. I had a modest scholarship to Grandview College in Des Moines, and I could have commuted back and forth, and found a part-time job to help supplement the costs. Student loans were not that hard to get back then. But in my mind, I knew I hadn't really prepared myself. Those last few years in high school it had been too easy. I could participate in sports and just scrape by with the classwork, and then look forward to my summer vacations. I guess, for me, it had been a very idyllic and predictable life, but that had all changed now. In another few weeks, I'd be turning 18, and I wasn't prepared, either mentally or emotionally, for college. For that matter, I wasn't ready to be an adult either, and that was just fine with me.

While I was sitting there daydreaming about whether I wanted to work or just play around for the summer, on the other side of the country, 1800 miles away, at Camp Pendleton in California, a seemingly low key event was taking place that would very shortly change the entire shape and direction of my life.

It was late spring of 1966, the 3rd Battalion, 26th Marine Regiment was being reactivated. It had been over 20 years since they had last seen action at Iwo Jima during WWII. They were first assembled in March of 1944, specifically for the assault on the Japanese held islands in the Pacific. Then the entire 26th Regiment was deactivated at the end of the war.

With the escalation of troop strengths in Vietnam in 1965, the 3rd Battalion, 26th Marines were once again being called up for war. In just seven months, after intensive training, they would be landing a BLT (Battalion Landing Force) in Vietnam, and building a small foothold of a combat base at Camp Evans (named after the first 3/26th Marine to die in Vietnam). In their first few weeks, right after landing, the newly arrived Marines would be attacked and probed relentlessly by companies of VC[11] and NVA, wanting to test them. But all that was in my future. Back in the late spring of 1966, when this all was just beginning, I had no conception that that kind of world even existed. Instead, I was sitting in my third-period study hall, trying to decide between whether to open up a book and start reading, or to lob a spit wad at the head of my good buddy Randy Pierce. I chose the spit wad, and Randy, at 6'5" and 250 lbs., chose to righteously pound me good when study hall was over. We were, after all, "best friends."

"The Buddy Plan"

High School graduation day finally arrived. I was fortunate enough to have found a job as a summer intern with the Colfax Post Office. I was working as a mail carrier on one of the two in-town mail routes. I'd only been on the job for a few weeks, and was just starting to think that college wasn't for me, and that this might be a good career.

My original plan had been to register for school in the early fall at Grandview College in Des Moines, but frankly, I wasn't at all sure I could even afford to go to Grandview. Like any typical 18-yr old, I decided to worry about that later. Heck, I had a good paying job for the summer, and if things worked out, the possibility of being offered a full-time position. At that point, college was starting to become an afterthought.

I hadn't been the best of students in high school, especially in my senior year. I found myself playing hooky a lot, just acting out, and basically being lazy. My grades had fallen off, and I was behind in

---

[11] Vietcong

most of my classes, but somehow the grades were still good enough for me to graduate. So, there I was, about to turn 18 years old, and really confused about what my next step would be. Then, life took a strange turn.

My Brother and I Join the Marine Corps

My younger brother Bob had also been having trouble in school. His teachers said he just wasn't applying himself. Mom, who was raising all five of us kids by herself, knew that Bob was smart enough … but she just wasn't sure how to turn him around.

Mom remembered that when Bob was 15, she had sent him to live with our Uncle Harold in California for a year. It was his freshman year in high school, and he had done well. Actually, he had done very well, both in academics and in sports. I can remember Mom showing me letters from his principal, and pictures from the local paper that our uncle Harold had clipped out. They showed Bob playing on both the football and basketball teams, and doing well academically. I was shocked. I always knew my younger brother was a tough little S.O.B., but it was difficult for me to picture him as an outstanding student and athlete. Still, you couldn't argue with the letters from his school principal, or his picture in their local sports pages.

Sadly, when Bob came back to Iowa the following year, he started to fall into his old habits. I think the fact that he had done so well in California was because he had more structure in his life, and he was able to stay focused. Coming back to Iowa and hanging out with the old crowd just let him slip back into old habits.

It was the beginning of summer, and I was now working at the post office. One evening, after supper, Bob announced to the family that "he had made the decision to join the Marine Corps." I didn't know what to say, I only knew that once Bob decided to do something, he was going to do it.

Bob was still only 16, but his birthday was next month, and he was insistent enough that he had somehow managed to talk our Mom into signing the papers he would need. I never asked her about it, but I imagine she was remembering the dramatic turnaround he had made his freshman year in California, and she hoped that maybe, just maybe, this would be another opportunity for him.

Bob didn't have a car, so I was to drive him into Des Moines to see the recruiter. When the day came, we got an early start. I'd never driven in the "big city" of Des Moines before, and I was worried I might get lost. However, we made good time, and arrived at the recruiting office around 9:30 in the morning. Our luck was holding, and we found a parking spot right next to the recruiter's office, which was located on the ground floor of the old Shoppe's Building in downtown Des Moines.

The office turned out to be just a single room. We walked in the front door, and there was a narrow, darkly lit hallway that trailed off to the right. The recruiter's office was pretty bare, with just two chairs in front of a desk, and a small table to its left that held some brochures and colorful flyers. A coat rack was in the corner, but other than that, the office was practically empty.

Behind the desk sat the biggest, scariest guy I had ever seen. He was probably in his late twenties, had a buzz top haircut, and was wearing a class-A uniform, which consisted of brown shirt and tie, a white web belt, and navy blue trousers, with a big red NCO stripe down the side. He had 3 stripes on his sleeve (which meant he was a sergeant) and two full rows of ribbons above the pocket of his shirt. This guy looked just like the Marine in the recruiting poster on the wall.

Bob and I stood stiffly in front of the two chairs. We were both nervous, so I started to speak first. But before I could say anything, the sergeant jumped up, came around the desk and started shaking both our hands. There was a great big smile on his face, like he was really glad to see us. He had us sit down, and after introducing himself, he said, "I can see right away that you two are brothers (pause), so, you both want to join the Marine Corps?"

I have only a vague memory of what transpired during the next hour (it's been nearly 50 years after all). I do remember saying to the recruiter, "No, no, I'm not the one who wants to enlist. I'm just the driver. It's my younger brother who wants to join." The recruiter just kept on talking, like he was reading from a script. It was like he hadn't heard a word I had said.

I'm guessing he probably did hear what I'd said, because suddenly, he changed tactics, and with a very concerned look on his face started telling us that there "might be a problem." Since Bob was still only 16, he said, the Marine Corps might not be able to take him. However, the recruiter said that he was absolutely certain that, *if we were both to join together, on the "Buddy Plan,"* he could get us in by pulling some strings and calling in some favors. Looking back, I realize that the only thing he was trying to pull was "the wool over our eyes"! *He was after the both of us*!

Time seemed to stand still. My head was spinning. They were both staring at me, first the recruiter with that big, fatherly smile on his face, and then Bob, who had a look of deep desperation, like it was now me who was holding his entire future in my hands.

When it was all over, and the smoke had cleared, I had given in to the recruiter's 'bullshit line," and to my brother's guilt trip. To make matters worse, I found myself actually thanking the recruiter (!) as we signed our letters of intent.[12] With that, we were told to report for our physicals and the induction ceremony four weeks later. Both of our birthdays were in July, and by that time, Bob would have turned 17, and I would have turned 18.

Passing the Physical

The next four weeks passed quickly, and then it was time to report to

---

[12] Enlistees signed up for a period of three or four years; draftees for two years. I enlisted for three years, and Bob, because of his age, had to enlist for four years.

the local induction center in Des Moines, where we would receive our physicals, participate in the swearing in ceremonies, and receive our orders to report for basic training at MCRD[13] in San Diego, California.

At the induction center, we found ourselves lined up with a group of about 120 young men who were going into various branches of the service. Of that number, 26 were going to the Marine Corps, and they had come from all over Iowa and parts of eastern Illinois. The primary reason for us to be there was to see if we could first pass the physical exams. I didn't expect that either Bob or I would have a problem, but I was wrong. After I had taken my eye exam, the doctor went over to talk to our recruiter. The two of them talked for a few minutes, and then, the next thing I knew, the sergeant told me to come with him. There was no explanation of any kind.

The recruiter and I got in his car, and he drove several miles through Des Moines, and we soon arrived at a small building that housed a private optometrist's office. We went inside, and he had me stay outside in the waiting room, while he went in to visit with the eye doctor. About 10 minutes later, he came back out with some papers in his hand. We got in his car and drove straight back to the induction center, where I rejoined the group of inductees who were waiting to be sworn in.

Evidently, the brief visit to the private eye doctor's office had resulted in some sort of magical improvement in my vision that was just short of being a miracle. It's amazing what they could do back then, just by changing some paperwork.

(That's the last I ever heard about the matter, except when I did eventually get fitted for eyeglasses at boot camp. The examiner there wondered aloud how I ever got past my initial physical. Even though the lenses in the glasses they issued to me were a little thick, I

---

[13] MCRD: Marines Corps Recruit Depot. There are only two in the U.S., one in San Diego and the second at Camp Lejeune in North Carolina. Everyone on the west side of the Mississippi goes to California; everyone on the east side goes to North Carolina.

noticed that a lot of new recruits in basic training had glasses thicker than mine.)

A couple of weeks after our physicals, Bob and I received our travel orders and vouchers for our expenses. We were to board a train in Des Moines that was bound for San Diego, California on July 26th, 1966. The trip would take two days, and our route would pass through El Paso, Texas, and then westward towards California.

Once on the train, we found that we had been assigned our own cabin with pull down bunks. The cabin featured a sink with running water, but we had to go outside the cabin to the next car to use a common restroom. Meals could be delivered to our cabin, and a conductor would stop by twice a day with a menu to see if we wanted to order from that, or just take our meals in the separate dining car. We would take most of our meals in the cabin, but occasionally, Bob would prefer to visit the dining car, where he found that he could order a beer with his meal. No one ever thought to ID Bob because he was a Marine Corps recruit. We had to pay for the alcoholic drinks out of our own pockets, so it was probably a good thing that neither of us had taken a lot of money with us.

There wasn't a lot to do while we were on the train, other than look out the windows and watch the scenery as it passed by. Bob had packed a deck of playing cards to help us 'while away the hours', but we soon came to realize that neither of us knew any card games other than just a bit of poker.

We would get into arguments about which poker hands had precedence beyond three of a kind. It almost turned into a fist fight when he decided to show me a new game he had just learned called "52 Card Pickup." The argument was about who was going to have to pick up the cards lying all over the floor. After a while, we both just settled in, and read magazines or took naps until it was mealtime.

The next two days passed monotonously slow. I do remember that when the train made a brief stop in El Paso, the temperature outside was 104 degrees. Air conditioning in our cabin didn't work so well, but at least we had shade, and could leave the windows open. We were glad to get moving once again, and when we finally arrived in San Diego, we both vowed to not ever take a train ride again[14]. I remember that our travel orders instructed us to wait just outside of the train depot area where we would find an alley way that had a sign saying, "MCRD Pickup". This stood for Marine Corps Recruit Depot, and that is where a bus finally picked up about an hour later.

There was a Corporal on the bus who checked our paperwork, but other than that, he didn't seem to have too much time to pay attention to our questions. He just motioned for us to find a seat and Bob and I settled into one of the back three rows. This was not what either of us had expected, and somehow it seemed anticlimactic. Could it be that everything we had read or heard about the Marine Corps was a complete exaggeration?

Another half hour, and we had reached our destination. The bus came to a stop, the door burst open, and the next thing I realized, the bus had been boarded by crazy people.

---

[14] As the years have passed, and I look back upon those times, I've come to view that three-day train ride Bob and I took a lot differently. Although I'm still not that enthusiastic about traveling by modern-day trains, if I had an opportunity to ride on one of the old passenger rail trains of that day, I think I would jump at the chance, just to experience the nostalgia all over again of those three days I spent with my younger brother.

Chapter 3

Basic Training

The subject of Marine Corps boot camp has probably been written about more than any other aspect of military service. The levels of physical hardship, the extent of weapons and martial arts training, and most especially, the mental discipline that is instilled in each Marine recruit has become legendary. Bob and I both came to find out that it was all true, although some of the more salient facts had been carefully left out when the recruiter was describing our basic training to us. If I remember correctly, our recruiter had assured us that the eight or nine weeks of boot camp training would just "breeze by" and the next thing we knew, we would be full-fledged Marines.

Dear Mom,   *7-30-1966*

Arrived safely and have been here 2 days so far. It has been rugged but I am sure that Bob and I can shape up. The D.I.'s treat us like dirt but we know that is just what they are supposed to do. I have only a few minutes and I should be cleaning and assembling my rifle. I will write more later.

Your son,
Bill

This is the first letter that I wrote to my Mom, just two days after arriving…

Normally, boot camp training was a 12 or 13-week process, but due to the escalation of troops to Vietnam in 1965, our training cycle had been shortened to just eight weeks. Looking back now at those first two weeks of boot camp, it's very much just a blur. I do remember that it was both a physical and psychological challenge.

Bob and I were both in good shape, so we were able to handle the physical aspect of the training, but the psychological stress was something totally new for both of us. I was worried about how Bob would handle all the yelling and "in your face" screaming, because he wasn't used to taking crap from anyone (the result of growing up with 2 older brothers). Surprisingly, Bob handled it in stride, and adapted to the training more easily than I did. I was used to trying my best all the time, and then getting praised for it right away. Bob, not so much. Ironically, this had made him mentally tougher from the very beginning, and it was something I was going to have to learn.

It would be many more weeks before anyone in our platoon would hear the words, "Good job Marine!"

These were pictures from our platoon yearbook, taken on the 2nd day of boot camp.

Everything about boot training is focused on transitioning the new recruits from acting as individuals to acting as part of a team, without hesitation, and with precision and confidence for completing their mission, no matter what it is. This doesn't happen overnight; it takes many long weeks of preparation and training. And it is intense.

There were three phases to Marine boot training: The initial training at the recruit depot; weapons and thorough marksmanship training at the rifle range; and finally, advanced recruit training back at the main depot. In all there were 11 areas of specialized training, focusing on us both as individuals and as a group. We had to complete all phases successfully before we would graduate from boot camp and become Marines.

There were four platoons in our training cycle, each comprised of 75 men, and these training platoons would make up a training company. Near the end of the 8-week training cycle, all four platoons competed fiercely in each of the 11 categories of testing to win the coveted *"Honor Platoon Banner."* Eventually, our Platoon, Platoon 1075, would win that banner by placing 1st in 10 of the 11 categories.

Rifle training is considered so critical to a Marine's recruit training that they spend two full weeks dedicated to nothing but that. I believe it was in the fifth and sixth week of our training cycle when we were all loaded aboard a bus and transported to Edson Range at Camp Pendleton. It was there that we were to receive thorough and intense training, and then, final qualification on the rifle range.

As long as a Marine is on active duty, they are required to periodically re-qualify with the rifle. Every Marine, no matter what his eventual assignment and duty station, will always be considered a rifleman, first and foremost. The Marine Corps takes this portion of the training *very* seriously.

The Rifle Range

As best as I can remember, the basic itinerary was pretty much the same every day: Get up early in the morning, go to chow, exercise, assemble for a 3-5 mile run, attend class instruction, go to mid-day chow, spend the rest of the afternoon in grueling rifle instruction courses, where we learned to aim and sight our targets, adjust rifle slings and mark the slings with how they should be positioned for firing in different situations.

There were three basic positions we learned to fire from: Standing, sitting, and the prone position for the most demanding firing distances at 500 yards. One of the first things they tell all recruits is that if you already know how to shoot a rifle it will probably take you longer to learn "the correct way, the Marine Corps way," which is a very precise process of adjusting the rifle sling and getting into such tight positions, sometimes for hours it seemed, learning to breathe correctly, and to control the body so that each shot is sent down range with precision. During training, we would sometimes be in shooting positions for hours, just sighting in with our steel sights on the bullseye, with the slings so tight that the pain on the body was almost unbearable.

A rifle instructor would sometimes test the integrity of our positions by kicking the front barrel of the rifle while we were in the sitting or prone positions. We would rock back and forth, but when we finally came to rest, the blade of the front sight was still sitting exactly on the bullseye of our targets. The training was excruciating, but the results made us realize how valuable it all really was.

Bob and I both may have had an advantage. We had been trained by our father, who was a rifle instructor in the Army, and one of the things he always emphasized was proper breathing. We were both pretty good marksmen when we entered the Marine Corps, but when we graduated from the rifle range, we were both at a whole new level.

One incident that happened at the Edson Rifle Range is worth mentioning. It was the final day of qualification. We were firing for the scores that would determine if we would individually be able to proceed with our platoon, or if we would be sent back and have to start all over again.

No one wanted to have to start over, but my brother Bob was having a problem. For some reason, he hadn't done so well at the shorter ranges, 200 and 300 yards, and he was in danger of not passing. That would also have brought down the overall platoon scores, and the

DI's[15] were not about to let that happen. While the rest of the platoon moved to the 500-yard distance, the DI's pulled Bob aside, and had a little chat with him. The "little chat" may have involved some form of "physical instruction," because he was a little wobbly on his way back.

Whatever they said to Bob, it had a really positive effect on him because he shot a perfect score from the 500-yard mark, ten bullseyes in a row, the best performance by anyone in our platoon at that distance. This helped Bob's total score, and it was now good enough for him to pass the rifle range requirements. It also gave our platoon enough points to win the battalion ribbon.

We had another 3 weeks of boot camp left. Everyone in the platoon was becoming adjusted to the rigorous training schedule. We were starting to look and feel like real Marines.

The Guamanians

Another incident of note happened about our third or fourth week of training. The head drill instructor, Staff/Sgt. Blue, had sent word that I was to report to his office. This was normally not a good thing, and I was very nervous when I knocked on his office door and requested permission to enter. After shouting out the standard military greeting ("Pvt. Ward reporting as ordered Staff/Sergeant!"), Sgt. Blue told me to "stand at ease."

While I stood there waiting, my mind was racing through all the possible reasons as to why I had been called in. Sgt. Blue finally lifted his head, and in a surprisingly gentle and normal voice (this actually scared me even more), "Pvt. Ward, I've got a bit of a situation here, and I want to ask you a favor. It's about the Guamanians."[16]

---

[15] Drill Instructors

[16] Background Note: Our training platoon consisted of 76 recruits, 13 of whom were volunteers from the island of Guam, which is a U.S. Territory. The social leader of their group was Francis Tydingo, who would later become one of my best friends.

Sgt. Blue continued, "There's been some reports that the Guamanians aren't being accepted very well by the other recruits, and for that reason, they're not blending in very well with the rest. That shit is going to stop! Now!" I could tell he was starting to boil over, then he abruptly eased back down. "I see where you and "Little Brother" (the nickname they had given to Bob) seem to get along with several of them. I want you to keep that up and try to get to know the rest of them. If you see any other scumbag recruits giving them any crap, I want you to say something." I answered, "Yes, Drill Sergeant!"

That's about as far as the conversation went, and then he abruptly dismissed me. I wasn't sure at all about what was going on, but I figured that it wouldn't be a problem. I was already getting to know several of them well, especially Francis Tydingo, who seemed to be their unofficial leader. When I got the first opportunity, I told Bob what Sgt. Blue had said to me.

Bob and I had both had been impressed with the Guamanians from the beginning. Although they were a bit stand-offish to everyone at first, they were, to a man, a tough and intelligent group of people, and it was not difficult for Bob and me to like them. Things did seem to improve after that. I think it was more due to the fact that everyone in the platoon began to see that the "Guamanians" were actually going to end up being good Marines.

Recruits That Fail to Pass Boot Camp

You might be wondering, when my brother and I went through boot camp, how many recruits actually graduated from a boot camp platoon. For the most part, they all did, unless there were extenuating circumstances, such as medical issues or otherwise. But still, at times, as many as 5-10% of new recruits might fail to measure up to the required standards, or worse, they might decide that they wanted

These are pictures of our platoon at the end of the 8-week training cycle. Our platoon, 1075, had won the overall regimental honor platoon flag and 10 of the possible 11 banners. Each banner was for an area we were tested in. In the pictures above, our lead drill instructor, Staff/Sergeant Blue, is pinning on the banner for winning the rifle training competition, which, along with close order drill, was probably the most prestigious of all the competitions.

to drop out. These Marines would have to go back and begin training all over, but before that happened, the Marine Corps has a special unit that they would send these people to. It was called the "Motivation Platoon." You did not want to go there.

The one thing the Marine Corps knows how to do, - better than any other branch of the service – is to motivate recruits, and they can keep you "motivating"[17] for as long as it takes to get your mind right. There is no easy way out, once you're assigned to the Motivation Platoon, where the intense physical and mental tasks you encountered each day were designed specifically to "get your mind right."

Punishment was rationed out for even the smallest of mistakes. Popular punishments were not always physical, for instance, you might be ordered to clean all the latrines, or a long stretch of sidewalk, with only a tooth brush, *your personal toothbrush*. All

---

[17] "Motivating" is a term that the drill instructors came up with that describes a condition of being in continuous motivation, like a man being chased by a raging bull.

physical conditioning drills were taken to new levels, but by far, the psychological motivation techniques were the worst, putting even the North Koreans to shame.[18]

One of our own, who I'll just refer to as "Pvt. Charles B.," was sent to the "Moto Platoon." He suffered from several deficiencies, which included; "fat body, weak body, lack of confidence, and a general malaise that seemed to extend to anyone who was standing next to him." He was, in short, a total, walking disaster, and why he ever thought he should (or could) join the Marine Corps in the first place was beyond understanding.

We pretty much lost track of Pvt. Charles B. after the rest of our platoon graduated, but I did hear once that he had been kept in the "Motivation Platoon" well beyond the normal period. I just assumed that he had failed and was finally given a "mercy discharge" from the service, but as it turned out, that was not the case. The truth was even stranger.

Towards the end of my enlistment (in 1969), I ran into several of my old buddies from boot camp, and they were telling me about a chance meeting they had had with Charles B. (now *Sergeant Charles B.*"). Evidently, after he finally was returned from Motivation Platoon to complete his basic boot camp training, he "breezed" through it. From there, he breezed through all the Advanced Infantry Training, and then was assigned to "Specialized Operations Training" and jump school. He finally ended up in Marine Corps Force Reconnaissance, the most elite of all Marine Corps operational units. These are the guys that can be dropped in behind enemy lines, with the sole purpose of assassination or elimination of specific targets. These were the shadow players in the Marine Corp's arsenal of weapons that they called out when they "absolutely, positively, needed someone killed today." These were the "baddest of the bad," and the Marine Corps' finest.

---

[18] Training of pilots for survival if they are shot down and captured is based on the methods employed by the North Korean to torture POWs.

I was glad to hear that Pvt. Charles B. had turned himself around, but I also wasn't really eager to get back together and talk about old times. It became clear to me that when the Marine Corps sends someone to the Motivation Platoon, they end up either having to release them from the service, or they get someone who is now a *highly motivated* Marine. They sometimes even get a "Sgt. Charles B."

After Boot Camp Came "Basic Infantry Training"

I remember going home for a 20-day leave after Basic Infantry Training in November of 1966. I had been hoping to take the last 10 days around Christmas[19], but that didn't work out. I'd made the mistake of signing a volunteer list to take six weeks of jungle warfare training in Okinawa with the 3rd Recon Training Battalion, and then go on from there to Vietnam. The extra month and a half in Okinawa would have counted against my 13-month Vietnam tour, and I figured it was better to be doing jungle training in Okinawa than actually being in Vietnam for those 45 days.

No such luck, as it turned out, they only had 15 Marines volunteer for Recon. They were originally looking for 20, so they still needed 5 more and they had to come back through the barracks, asking for more volunteers. They finally got all the volunteers they needed, and so, with a few misgivings, but also with the sense that this was going to be an adventure, I left my name on the list. When I came back from leave, I received my new orders and also a final date telling me when we would be boarding the transport ship for Vietnam.

We would be leaving aboard the USS Walker on January 4, 1967. I, along with the other 19 volunteers for Recon training, would be dropped off in Okinawa (approximately 19 days out) and the remaining troops would arrive in Vietnam in 21 days.

---

[19] All Marines get 30-days leave per year. Bob and I had joined the service mid-year. Our first opportunity to take any part of that 30 days wouldn't happen until after boot camp. I was trying to finesse a 20-day leave, then another 10-day leave around Christmas, but that didn't work out as I had planned, and I effectively lost those last 10 days of leave.

[This is a letter to mom, sent 10-6-1966, after graduating from boot camp.]

Dear Mom,

My new address is "C-2 Company, 1ˢᵗ Btn, 2ʳᵈ ITR (that stands for Infantry Training Regiment). We're here at Camp Pendleton now and boy is it a big place. If you get a letter from Bob please send me his address because they separated us right after boot camp. I can't figure that out. They promised to keep us together through our training when we signed up on the "buddy plan".

We've been out training in the field all his last week. They even set up temporary mess halls out there to give us 1 hot meal a day. So far the only weapon's training, besides our rifles, has been with the 81mm mortars and the M-79 grenade launchers. I get a kick out of shooting those old WWII M-1's, half of them are ready for the scrap heap. We'll get our new M-14's before we leave for overseas.

....

I don't actually dislike the field training. Sometimes it's fun. Yesterday we were simulating climbing cliffs and had to crawl up a 30-foot rope to a scaling tower. When I got to the top, the training officer actually said, "Good job!" When I realized he was talking to me I almost fell off the tower. We're not used to hearing things like that during training.

...

I get 30 days leave before going overseas so I'll try to get it after this training. When we finish ITR I have to go for an additional 14 days of Advanced Infantry Training, then I should be able to come home on leave.

    Love,
    Bill

Chapter 4

21 Days at Sea

The day finally came for us to begin our departure for Vietnam. Right after morning chow, we were assembled and loaded onto transport vehicles, which were actually just converted cattle car carriers[20]. They had wood planks on the floor, no seats, you just had to find something to hang onto all the way from Camp Pendleton down to the San Diego docks, where we assembled with all our gear to wait for our orders to start boarding the troop transport ship USS Walker.

The Walker was going to transport a contingent of 2,200, freshly trained Marines to Danang harbor. There would be short refueling stops at Pearl Harbor, Okinawa, and then the final three-day leg of the trip before we landed in Vietnam.

---

[20] These were specially converted troop transportation that was used within the U.S. and were originally designed for transporting cattle. See more information in **Chapter Notes** (Chapter 4) at the end of this book.

I can still remember standing on that pier in San Diego, watching an unending line of Marines with duffle bags slung over their shoulders, walking slowly up the gang planks. It took most of the afternoon to geteveryone on board. About halfway through the process, I could see some of the new recruits were starting to get seasick, right on the gang plank to the ship. They hadn't even boarded the ship yet. I think it must have been a combination of being excited, standing all day out in the hot sun. The smell that started to drift into the air, as more and more recruits started to succumb, only made it worse.

I wasn't immune either, and I started to feel seasick almost right away. It would be another seven days before I finally got my "sea legs," and for that time, I have almost no memories whatsoever of being onboard, except for being placed in a small, cramped bunk below decks with everyone else who was sick.

I vaguely remember one of the Staff Sergeants who would check on me from time to time, and how he would try to get me to eat some crackers and drink a little water. Most everyone else started to recover within a day or two, but there were some of us who had it really bad, and we were just left in our bunks, near the head[21] and the showers, until we finally recovered. There was really nowhere else to put us, because the sickbay area was completely filled.

From time to time, I was helped topside to get some fresh air, but it wasn't until around the 6th day that I was able to go topside on my own. It was midmorning, and I could see hundreds of Marines on deck, engaged in calisthentics, cleaning their gear, or just sitting around. I had no idea where my group was, or what they were doing. I had completely fallen "off the radar," and I didn't even know who I was to report to.

Finally, I started feelng well enough to start thinking about food. I had gone so long without any real food that I didn't feel hunger so much as just an emptiness in my stomach, and a total weakness and exhaustion in my body. And then, I started to smell food. The smell

---

[21] The "head" is the name given to the bathroom facilities.

was coming from down below decks, and there was a long line of Marines going through a hatch door topside. I got in line and followed them down to the mess hall. Once I finished eating, I went back up on deck, waited about 15 minutes, and thengot back in line again.

As I mentioned, I had long since lost touch with whatever structural command I had been assigned to, and for the next week, my schedule was to go topside, watch all the other Marines going to and from their assigned activities, while I just took in the fresh, salt air. After a while, I'd get in a chow line, have something to eat, and then repeat the process until I'd had four or five meals. I'd then go below when it was time to sleep. Whatever temporary group I had been assigned to, they had long ago forgotten about me, and I was in no great hurry to become reunited with them.

Eventually, I did start to get bored with this routine. I started asking some questions, and after a short time ,I did find my temporary unit. I got back into a regular routine of morning calesthetics, training, chow line, and a lot of personal time when we had an opportunity to stay above decks and explore the ship. Sometimes, I would just stare out at the sea and watch as waves passed by. I was a long way from Iowa.

About the 10th day out we were due to cross the international dateline, which means we would lose a calendar day. It also meant that there was an initiation that all of us had to endure.

A "polywog" is someone who has never crossed the international dateline before. (There's a similar ceremony for crossing the equator.) It is where all the "polywogs" have to get into a line and subject themselves to all kinds of indingnities; the worst being having to crawl on our hands and knees down a line, as someone (a "Shellback." i.e., someone who had crossed the line before) would pour the most disgusting concoction of foul smelling liquids all over the top of your head. All you could do was hold your nose and hope to not throw up. Then, you had to perform all the trivial and meaningless little tasks they could dream up for our torment and their entertainment. Finally, mercifully, they let us run below decks to the showers and clean ourselves off. And now, we, too, were "Shellbacks."

We had at least another good 10 days at sea before we would arrive in Vietnam. It seemed to get warmer after that. I guess we were getting closer to the equator.

I started to find it was more difficult to get to sleep at night, and that's when I started to notice all the graffiti that was scribbled on the undersides of each bunk. It seemed that almost every bunk had something written, or drawn, on the underside of the bunk canvas. All I can remember about the drawings on the bunk above me was that someone had drawn a calendar, and they had been marking off the days while they were at sea. Another drawing was of a palm tree on a beach, with waves lapping at the shore. Evidently that anonymous artist must have felt that they were going to some kind of tropical paradise. In a different time, he might have been right.

I decided against writing anything on the canvas above my head. I wanted to write "Bill Ward was here! January 15th, 1967," but then I had a flashback to seven months prior, when I was about to graduate high school, and our principal, Mr. Murdock, caught me writing graffiti on the locker room wall. He chewed me out pretty good for that, and I guess the lesson stuck, because I ended up not writing anything on the bunk canvas. In so doing, I missed an opportunity of a lifetime to have my name, along with audio and video recordings about that experience, enshrined in the archives at the Smithsonian Institute, the Library of Congress, and another half dozen smaller museums dedicated to preserving historical and military artifacts. Here's the story about this bunk graffiti:[22]

The Vietnam Graffiti Project:

Jack Fisk, the production designer for the film "The Thin Red Line" had contacted the Maritime Administration to locate a troop

---

[22] With the kind permission of the "Vietnam Graffiti Project" (www.vietnamgraffiti.com)

transport ship so he could film its architectural details, prior to construction of a film set. Keswick, Virginia neighbor Art Beltrone, a military artifact historian, was advising on the historically correct weapons, uniforms and equipment used by the Army troops during their 1942 fighting on Guadalcanal.

Jack learned there was a troopship in Virginia's James River Reserve Fleet that contained intact berthing compartments and galleys, and an almost functional bridge and power plant. The ship was the General Nelson M. Walker, a vessel capable of carrying as many as 5,000 troops. Permission was granted for a visit to both Jack and his neighbor.

On a chilly February morning, Fisk and Beltrone were guided through the Walker, and the production designer began filming the ship's interior. In the first troop compartment they entered, they felt as if they had entered a time capsule. There, on the seemingly endless bunks, stacked four-high, were original pillows, sheets, blankets and bright orange life vests.

It was at that moment both visitors encountered what would become a fascinating piece of American military history. One that would ultimately become a lasting tribute to the Americans who served in Vietnam. On the underside of many canvas bunk inserts were graffiti drawings and messages, written mostly with black felt tip pens by troops going to Southeast Asia in 1966 and 1967. Similar messages were found throughout the ship's other troop compartments on several deck levels.

The discovery of the graffiti and other artifacts led to a project to recover the material for preservation in museums throughout the country. Beltrone and his wife Lee formed the non-profit "Vietnam Graffiti Project." and with other volunteers, worked with the Maritime Administration and museums to remove examples of the historic material and relocate the artifacts to American repositories and museums. Among the recipients—the Library of Congress, Smithsonian Institution, museums operated by the United States Army, Navy and Marine Corps, and state and local museums throughout the country, have done considerable research of the names on the canvases, and this has led to finding many of the veterans who originally created the graffiti, and audio interviews were conducted to preserve their stories of the voyage.

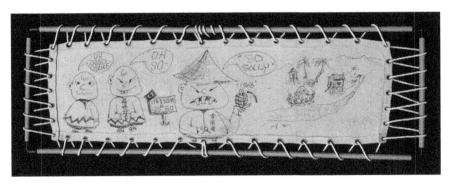

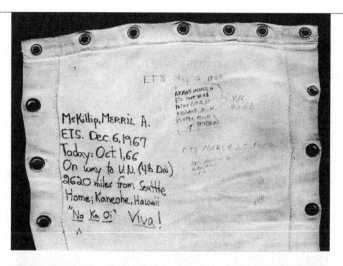

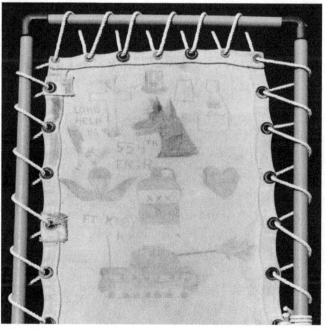

Chapter 5

Arriving in Danang

In another few days we would be in Vietnam. Tomorrow we were to stop at Okinawa, and once again, I was told that my orders had been changed. I had had been preparing to debark, with 19 other Marines, to begin training with the 3rd Division's 3rd Recon Battalion, A Co., at Camp Schwab, once we reached Okinawa. I now found out that a new group of 20 volunteers had been flown directly over to Vietnam, by commercial airline from the states, and that I and the other 19 volunteers onboard the Walker, were now going to continue on with the rest of the troops, and that I would be assigned to the 2nd Battalion, 26th Marines when we arrived in Danang. I wrote a letter to Mom about this time, telling her about all the assignment changes, but that I was happy at least to have my final orders. As it would turn out, the Marine Corps was yet done shuffling me around. I would not end up with the 2nd Battalion, 26th Marines.

When we finally arrived in Danang Harbor, all troops and gear were off-loaded. The group I was with was transported by truck to an airstrip in Danang, where we waited in the hot afternoon sun, sitting on our sea bags at the edge of the tarmac. We were all wondering what was going to happen next. Two hours later, we were shuffled onto helicopters and flown the 40-mile flight north to Phu Bai[23], which was just south of Hue, the old capital city.

We arrived in Phu Bai. It was getting to be early evening by now. We were all led to a large tent that was serving as a temporary chow hall. About the only thing I can remember from that experience was that they had a milk machine in their mess hall that dispensed both

[23] Phu Bai Combat Base (also known as Phu Bai Airfield and Camp Hochmuth) is a former U.S. Army and U.S. Marine Corps base south of Hué in Central Vietnam. It was also headquarters for the 3rd Marine Division.

white and chocolate milk[24].

When we finished, half of our group stayed at Phu Bai, and the other half (the group I was in) were loaded back onto the helicopters for another ride to Camp Evans, which was located north of Phu Bai.

Welcome to Camp Evans

So there I was, my first night in Vietnam, and I was finally with my assigned unit[25]. I still hadn't been told what company or platoon I would be assigned to, but at that moment, my most immediate concern was where I was going to sleep that night. It was dark now, and the constant drizzle of rain was starting to turn the ground into a muddy, slippery mess. I could see several larger tents towards the middle of the camp, but they didn't seem to be occupied by troops, so I assumed they were for supplies and storage.

Just then, an older corporal (who I later found out to be Cpl. Rhett Holley), who was maybe 23 or 24 years old, walked up and directed us to follow him. Besides being dark, it was surprisingly chilly. The light drizzle continued to fall as we made our way towards a series of roughly constructed sand bag bunkers, which were just behind the fox holes and barb wire that made up the security perimeter of the camp.

Making our way in the dark was difficult. I was carrying my rifle and all my possessions in a large canvas sea bag, trying to navigate around the sand bag bunkers, crates of equipment, and supplies. Finally, we came to the bunker where I was to spend the night. Corporal Holley yelled inside the bunker, and soon, three Marines

---

[24] When the Army originally built the Phu Bai base, it included many amenities that the average Marine was unaccustomed to seeing.

[25] The "3/26th"; 3rd Battalion, 26th Marine Regiment, had been shipped over to Vietnam as an entire BLT (Battalion Landing Team) on December 12th, 1966, 6 weeks before I arrived with a small group of replacements.

scrambled outside. He said to them, "This is Pfc. Ward [26], a new replacement. He'll be bunking with you tonight until we get him squared away in the morning," and with that, he turned and left.

I stood there, waiting for someone to tell me what to do next, or at least for someone to introduce themselves, but instead, the three Marines just crawled back inside their bunker without a word. I couldn't just stand out there in the drizzling rain, so I crawled in behind them, dragging my sea bag through the mud, while I tried to wrestle it inside the small opening that was used as a door.

Once inside, I was surprised to see that there was a little more floor space than I had anticipated, but the ceiling was very low, and there was barely room to sit up. The three Marines had already settled in for the night. One was curled up in his poncho in the corner and the other two were sitting, trying to sleep, with their backs against the far wall. That left nearly half the floor space for me to find a place to sleep.

The floor at my end of the bunker was sunken a little lower because of the slope of the hill we were on, so I decided to dig into my sea bag and pull out the rubber air mattress that I had been issued as part of my overseas gear. It took a while to blow up the mattress, but when I was finally done, and I had laid it down on the mud floor, it was really quite comfortable. I looked again at the other three guys, who were scrunched up on the back half of the bunker. Surprisingly, I had plenty of room on my half of the floor, so I didn't worry about it, and decided I'd just try to get some sleep. Morning was going to come soon enough.

It started raining harder as the night progressed, but I didn't notice that as I slept away on my new air mattress. But, that would only last for a few hours. I suddenly woke up with a start. I sensed that something was wrong. The mattress was moving, slowly at first, and then a little faster. I looked up to see what was happening, and that's

26 A Pfc. is a Private First Class (E-2)

when I saw that the two Marines who had been sleeping with their backs to the wall were now sitting up, staring directly at me, and one of them was even saluting, while my mattress, with me on it, slowly floated out the front door and into the rain.

It was pouring, and I was getting drenched. I scrambled to get back inside. I now saw that the lower half of the bunker, where I had been sleeping, was a rushing stream of water. As I was to later learn, when the rain starts to pick up, all that extra water flows downhill and seeps between the sand bags. Then it looks for the lowest part of the floor, which, tonight, was where I was sleeping, and it would spill outside to continue on its journey downhill.

Now I realized why the other three guys were all hunched up on the higher part of the bunker floor. Still, it didn't explain why no one had bothered to tell me. Then I remembered the strange sight of the one Marine, just a few minutes ago, sitting straight up and saluting as I floated out the door, and INTO THE RAIN! They all knew exactly what was going to happen. I guess they just wanted me to experience it for myself. It was my first lesson in surviving in Vietnam: "If it's raining, stay on the higher ground."

I had left the air mattress outside, and for now, just looked for a dry spot on the upper (higher) half of the bunker floor. Then I covered up with my poncho. Everyone still seemed to be asleep (or at least pretending to be), which was just as well, because there was no way in hell I was going to give them the satisfaction of hearing me complain. Besides, these guys were rough looking, bad smelling, combat-hardened veterans, and I was just the new guy, fresh from the States. Before I finally fell off to sleep again, I had this weird feeling that I was going to like these guys.

[L-R: Harland, Bill Halsey, Rhett Holley, George Eriksson...] *Cpl. Holley was our fire team leader, and would later be promoted to Sergeant and squad leader.*

[This article is from "The Sea Tiger" a newspaper which was written and printed by the III MAF (3rd Marine Amphibious Force) exclusively for use by all the units that were operating in the I-Corps area of Vietnam. The I-Corps area was the northern most operational area in South Vietnam, operating predominately between Danang and the DMZ to the north.]

Operation Chinook:

Three rugged days before truce began

By: Cpl. Cal Guthrie

PHU BAI—Waves of Viet Cong soldiers moving behind barrages of enemy mortars pounded Marine lines from dusk to dawn marking the last day of fighting on Operation Chinook before the Christmas truce.

The 3rd Battalion, Twenty-Sixth Regiment, 3rd Division Marines killed more than 30 communist soldiers during the nightlong battle. This brought the enemy dead total to 154 in three days of fighting.

Marine casualties were light.

More than 400 rounds of enemy mortar fire pounded the Marine positions during the action, starting at dusk on Dec. 23 and continuing through the early morning hours of Christmas Eve. The communists broke contact and fled at dawn.

Fighting from water-filled holes in torrential rains during the all-night engagement, the Marines drove back an estimated three companies of hard-core VC.

The communists came within 10 yards of the Marine lines at times in attempts to overrun the positions.

A flareship was on station in an attempt to illuminate the bat-tlefield, but thick cloud cover hampered efforts. Marine artillery illumination was fired below the clouds and the battleground suddenly lit up catching enemy soldiers in the open. Rifles and machineguns caught them in a deadly cross-fire as they scurried for cover.

The grey light of dawn uncovered bodies, weapons, blood trails and blood-soaked rags littering the crater-pocked battlefront as the Marines moved through the area.

It ended the third such engagement in as many nights since the battalion took up positions in the rolling hills 12 miles north of Hue.

The battalion had been in Vietnam only two weeks when Operation Chinook began. They have become battle-tested veterans in a hurry.

At the end of three days of intense fighting the Marines have averaged more than 50 enemy kills a day. They captured five Viet Cong and seized more than 40 automatic weapons and light machineguns.

More than 200 Chinese communist-type grenades have been

(Continued on Back Page)

Chinook—

(Continued From Page 1)

taken from enemy bodies and several rice caches have been seized and destroyed.

"I" Co. alone accounted for more than 50 of the total enemy kills during three hours of savage fighting on the second night of the operation.

As the Christmas truce brought a lull in the fighting, the Marines bailed out their fighting holes, reinforced their positions and tried to catch some needed sleep.

My First Day with My New Unit

That next morning, I was sent up to the company supply tent to pick up whatever gear or supplies I would need for the next few days in the field. Among other things, this included 400 rounds of 7.62 ammunition for my M-14, a grenade pouch and 3 M-26 grenades, a flak jacket, mosquito repellent, canteen, Halizone water purification tablets, and Quinine tablets to prevent malaria. Everything else I pretty much had in my sea bag from when I had boarded the ship in San Diego. Finally, I was told to draw a 6-day supply of C-rations (we would consume 2 boxes per day), because we would be going out in the field in the next 10 hours on a night patrol.

When I got back to the bunker, Cpl. Holley was there to give me my assignment. I was to join one of the four-man fire teams in his 3rd squad, which was part of the 3rd platoon of Mike Company.[27] He formally introduced me to my bunk mates from the previous evening, Eriksson, Halsey, and Harland, and he made a specific point of telling me to "Watch Eriksson and Halsey, do what they do, learn to walk the way they walk, and, most importantly, keep my eyes open and my mouth shut." And then he added, "And if you're real lucky, you might just make it home alive."

The rest of the morning and afternoon were spent getting ready for our night patrol, which would kick off at 1800 (6 P.M.).[28] I had no idea what we would be doing, or how long we would be out, so I set about getting something to eat, because I hadn't had anything since the night before at Phu Bai.

---

[27] A more detailed description of USMC (and, NVA) unit structure can be found in the back of the book.

[28] Military Time is based on a 24-hour clock. "0800" ("zero eight hundred") is 8:00 a.m., and "1600" ("sixteen hundred") is 4:00 p.m.

There was no chow hall or temporary kitchens set up at Camp Evans. We basically just found a place to sit down, and opened up a box of C-rations. I had 12 boxes to choose from, so I started looking through my choices, and finally picked one that said "Ham & Lima

Beans." Probably the worst choice I could have made, but I was starving, so I just opened the box and started pulling everything out.

If memory serves, it consisted of one tin of ham and lima beans, a small package of crackers, some kind of cheese spread, and a can of fruit cocktail for desert. Along with that there was an accessory pack that had a plastic spoon, a P-38 can opener, a heat tablet for cooking the ham and beans, and a small four-pack of cigarettes. (Usually, Lucky Strikes, Camels, or Pall Malls).

By the time I finished the ham and beans, I'd pretty much lost my appetite for food, but the fruit cocktail turned out to be pretty good.

After the quick meal, I set about cleaning my rifle and packing my gear. I knew how to clean my rifle. Every Marine, whether he be a cook, a driver, a clerk, or a rifleman, has to first pass through initial rifle training, where he learns to disassemble and reassemble his rifle BINDFOLDED! That same Marine next has to qualify at the rifle range, shooting at ranges of 200, 300, and 500 yards, and they must meet the most demanding requirements any of the military branches. All Marines have to do this annually.

As I looked around at the other Marines who were packing their gear, I noticed that they were paying as much attention to their rifles as well as their packs. What you needed to carry in your pack or pockets depends on the type of mission you were going on and tonight's mission was going to be a simple overnighter.

Our 3rd platoon would roll out just after dark, go to a pre-arranged position (usually no more than 200-300 meters from the perimeter of the camp), and set up a night-long ambush along one of the trails leading into our camp. Aside from the one main supply road, there were numerous jungle trails that could be accessed to reach the camp. Our company headquarters would decide which ones we would be covering that night. In the morning, just before dawn, we would make our way back inside the perimeter, hopefully without being noticed by anyone observing the camp from a distance.

With all that in mind, I still had to decide what to put in my pack. Marines are taught by their squad leaders, and then they find out for themselves what works best. It really comes down to what you're willing to carry in order to be prepared for whatever you might encounter. It's quite an art in itself and everyone packs a little differently. For most everyone, there's a "must have" list of items: Extra ammunition, grenades, mosquito repellent, Quinine pills, Halizone tablets, and a poncho. But by far, the most variable item to go inside your pack were your C-rations.

Each box of C-rations weighed about two pounds, and provided approximately 1200 calories. Ideally you would carry two for each day (a total of 2400 calories), which was, at best, a minimal amount, because you could be burning as much as 5 to 10 thousand calories a day in jungle warfare conditions.

What a lot of people did not realize was that C-rations were always intended to be a short-term ration, designed for three days of maximum consumption before troops were given hot, freshly cooked meals. Intentions aside, in Vietnam, it was not unusual to spend five days in the field, eating nothing but C-rations. If you were going to

be there longer, resupply (usually by helicopter) was absolutely necessary. Luckily, tonight's mission was a short one, and I only packed a few carefully chosen items out of a single C-ration box.

Cpl. Holley's squad, with a machine gun team (total about 14 Marines), had been chosen to go outside the perimeter for this nighttime ambush. When the time came to assemble, we lined up near the south side of the camp. This confused me, because, except for the main road entrance, the entire perimeter was surrounded by concertina wire, which is a type of barbed or razor wire formed in large coils which can be expanded and stretched like a concertina (accordion). Triple concertina wire fences consist of two parallel concertinas, joined by twists of wire and capped with a third roll of concertina on top.

Heading Out

So, there we were, formed up in a long, single line, pointed directly at a wall of razor sharp concertina wire, and it was getting dark. Our squad leader, Cpl. Holley, walking to the front of the line, gave us these instructions, "No noise. Everyone line up behind me, and step where I step."

I wanted to turn and ask someone what was happening, but everyone's eyes were down, looking at the feet of the man in front of him. We weren't going to walk directly into the concertina? Were we?

I turned back to see where our squad leader was at and was astonished to see that he was standing in front of the wire, carefully lifting up his right leg. Then he positioned it on the front part of the coiled concertina, and stepped forward into it. The front edge of the wire fence flattened out against the ground, and the coiled razor wire barrier folded, ever so slightly, in front of him. No one in the line had moved a muscle or made a noise. Then he lifted his left leg, and did the very same thing again, moving even further into the concertina wire fence.

When he lifted his right leg again, I was startled to see the whole line of Marines in front of me move in perfect unison to his step. I even found that I had moved my right leg as well, without being told to, and without having the foggiest notion of why. The line continued moving forward in this strange manner, and soon there were three men inside the concertina entrapment. When it was my turn, I placed my right foot down on the wire, exactly where the right foot of the man in front of me was lifting his, and then continued on in the same way, placing my foot where his had just been.

When I finally crossed through the concertina barrier and was on the other side, I turned to look at the back of the line still coming through. It seemed almost surreal, like I was watching a line dance in slow motion, but without the music, executed in perfect silence. When the last man came through the wire, I watched as the concertina wire billowed back up behind him into its original shape. I was awestruck by what had just happened.

However, there was no time to think about it right then; we still had to hike to our night time ambush positions and get set up. Only later, when we were settled in for the long night's vigil, did I think back to it, and I remembered the very first instructions that I was given, "Watch these guys, and move like they move." It was good advice.

Several months later I'd get another reminder of Cpl. Holley's initial instructions. We were in the hills near the Khe Sanh[29] combat base, moving through high elephant grass. It was saturated with water from a recent rain storm, and I was getting soaked as I pushed my way through it. I noticed the guys in front of me weren't nearly as wet as I was, and I wondered why that was. Then I noticed that they were walking differently, almost crab-like, as they'd turn side to side, gliding through the grass, and in so doing, barely moving against it at all. It turns out that this was a trick they had learned by watching the Vietnamese. These were skills they'd never taught us back in our basic training.

The night patrol went off without incident. I distinctly remember feeling like Vietnam must be the coldest place on earth. We were wet from a constant, drizzling rain, and the nighttime temperatures dropped nearly 30 degrees from the daytime. We re-assembled in the morning and headed back to Camp Evans. We had to wait for about an hour before going back in, because the camp was receiving harassing mortar fire from the southeast. I still remember that night being one of the longest, coldest nights of my life, and just a taste of what was to come.

---

[29] The large Khe Sanh combat base was located north and west of Phu Bai and Camp Evans and close to the DMZ and to the South Vietnam/Laos border.

Learning the Trade

The next two weeks seemed to fly by quickly. I discovered that although my unit was the 3rd Battalion, which consisted of four rifle companies (India, Kilo, Lima, and Mike), each company operated in an independent manner. Battalion headquarters would rarely have two companies doing the same thing, in the same place, at the same time. If Mike Company was sent out into the field to do a sweep operation, Lima Company might also, but it would be in a different location, albeit close enough to provide support if either one got into some trouble.

At the same time, Kilo Company might be tasked with providing perimeter security around the base, while India Company would be assigned to Road Runner or Sparrow Hawk[30] duty. The one good thing about Sparrow Hawk duty was that you had plenty of time to catch up on your rest or letter writing. You could even roam around the base a bit, but the down side was that you had to get the "OK" from your squad leader first. We were required to be able to get back, grab our field gear, and be on the helipad in 15 minutes if there were an emergency and we had to be flown into the field.

For the first two weeks, it seemed that Mike Company was spending almost all its time in the field. This is a copy of a letter I wrote to my Mom on February 6, 1967, about two weeks after I had arrived in country. We were involved with Operation Chinook which was designed to clear the VC out of the local area. The sweep operations we were using in Operation Chinook were actually called "Sweep and Destroy," because, after relocating all the local farmers from their villages, we would not only destroy the villages, we would kill everything that moved, including the animals.

---

[30] "Road Runner" meant providing truck convoy security, and "Sparrow Hawk" means being left back at the base, inside the perimeter, in a quasi-state of readiness where we could be sent almost anywhere on a 15-minutes notice.

It struck me as being a very drastic tactic, but it was also effective in starving out the VC, especially those that were staged in large concentrations. I suppose it made more sense because we were in the northern most province of South Vietnam (Quang Tri), and this is where the NVA began moving their troops south, in preparation for the combined assaults they planned on launching against the larger southern cities like Hue and Danang, and eventually Saigon, which is much further south.

Still, it seemed to me to be very unfair to the Vietnamese people. Although they would be relocated to a safer place farther south, and were paid something for their livestock and possessions, I don't know how they would be able survive, other than waiting until the fighting was all over, and then returning to their old farms and rebuilding everything from scratch. [31]

Besides the constant fear of invasion from the North, the typical Vietnamese peasant farmer had to also contend with the local Viet Cong instigating terror and intimidation, demanding protection payments, stealing their rice, and conscripting their young men. In addition, there were local militias[32] (basically, armed local gangs and hooligans that would demand protection money from the villages and would act much like the old Mafia gangs would in the big cities back home.)

The biggest fear for the peasants was of the North Vietnamese coming across the DMZ and "liberating" vast areas of the South. They would take away all control of the farmland from the peasant farmers who had been working the land for generations. There were even rumors that many of the educated people in the village, especially teachers and town elders, would be charged as

---

[31] For an interesting perspective of the effect on the people of Vietnam of the decades of war with both the French and with the Americans, read a novel by David Lucas, "Uprooted – A Vietnamese Family's Journey, 1935-1975."

[32] The "local militias" were ostensibly set up to protect the villages from Viet Cong intimidation, but in reality, were simply providing protection from themselves. ("Uprooted, A Vietnamese Family's Journey – 1935 – 1975").

"capitalists" or trouble makers. This would mean being sent to indoctrination centers in the North, or even execution.

During my tour of duty in Vietnam, I was almost completely unaware of all of the politics involved, or what the local peasants had to endure. I often found myself confused by the wary and distrustful stares we would get when we encountered men, women, and children working in the fields, or when we walked through some of the smaller, isolated villages. I used to believe that it was simply because they were uneducated peasants who didn't understand why we were here. In fact, even the poorer Vietnamese in the countryside had strong family values and education, and worked very hard to make sure their children had time for school, even if it meant they could only work a half day in the fields[33]. In the evenings, after the family meal, adults would gather and discuss the swirl of local and national politics that engulfed them, and wonder about their futures. Their fears were not so much of Americans, but rather that, one day, the Americans would leave, and that anyone who had cooperated with them would be severely punished.

In the larger cities, such as Hue or Danang, the Vietnamese seemed more receptive to our presence than they normally did in the countryside. On the other hand, almost universally, we found the vast majority of young children to be delighted to see us. Sometimes we would give them treats, and, when time and circumstances permitted, we would take time to talk or even play with the children. This went a long way towards making the adults and village elders more inclined to talk with us.

---

[33] From "Uprooted, A Vietnamese Family's Journey – 1935 – 1975", by David Lucas

[The above picture is of my squad leader, Sgt. Rhett Holley. If we were around a village and had a little down time, he would never miss an opportunity to play with the children. This surprised me at first, because he was a "by the book" and "tough as they come" Marine, but he knew how to talk to the people. This had the added benefit of putting the villagers more at ease, and we often times would get information about local VC activity that might not have been so forthcoming otherwise. In the picture below, he is talking to one of the village elders.]

Chapter 6

February 1967 – A Long, Hard Month

February was my first, full month in Vietnam, and our time was spent mostly in the field, with occasional breaks back in camp at Camp Evans. We were still working under Operation Chinook guidelines and our mission was to sweep the areas throughout the Thua Thien Province, which included the old Capital City of Hue.

Camp Evans, our temporary home, was a rugged outpost; not much more than a few tents surrounded by sandbagged bunkers and fighting holes placed on the perimeter. It was named after Lance Corporal Paul Evans, the first member of 3/26 who was killed in Vietnam during the initial few days leading up to the Christmas truce.

My memories of the February, 1967 timeframe have been pretty vague. For the most part, I can just remember that it was my first full month in Vietnam. We were out in the field a lot, and starting to concentrate on going into the hills, searching out concentrations of VC who had been driven there by our sweeps of the valleys.

I also remembered that this was when I got my first experience with landmines and booby traps. We were venturing farther into the jungles and hills where "Charlie"[34] was hiding and my platoon was starting to encounter them a lot more often now. Sometimes I would just hear a distant explosion when one of the other platoons accidently set one off. Sometimes they were loud and booming when someone in my own platoon would set off a trip wire.

The VC were experts at finding our unexploded ordinance, like 250 lb. and 500 lb. bombs, and then burying them alongside a trail, connected to a trip wire. The VC would also plant Chicom[35] grenades inside of tins cans and leave them lying alongside the road. It was well known that Americans would kick at a loose can or box that they would see lying on the ground. Many times the smaller booby traps would only wound or maim a Marine, but it had the added benefit to the VC that it would then take two Marines to carry the wounded man back. The larger ordinance, however, such as unexploded bombs or rockets, would kill as many servicemen as they wounded.

When I looked back over the Command Chronologies for my company during the February time frame, it became obvious that we were encountering booby traps on almost a daily basis. In particular, I remember an incident where my platoon was going down a jungle trail. I had just walked past a spot in the trail, and just seconds later, there was a grenade blast that severely wounded the man who was behind me. I always felt that I must have been the one who "tripped the wire", and that the time delay set the grenade off when the next man walked by.

Normally we would all stay spaced at least five meters apart, but it was hard to gauge how long the fuses would burn before exploding. I was walking in the middle of the patrol, so that still didn't explain why no one else had set it off. Sometimes things just happen by pure

---

[34] "Charlie" was the "affectionate" nickname that was given to the Viet Cong.

[35] "Chicom" was short for "Chinese Communist."

chance, good or bad, and there's little control you have over the situation. In any case, it shook me up pretty bad at the time, and I was very careful to pay attention to where I put my feet after that.

Walking Point

I'd been in-country for about three weeks now with the 3rd platoon. We'd experienced sniper fire, incoming mortar barrages, and had set up a number of nighttime ambush positions while out in the field. I was starting to settle into the routine.

My primary MOS (Military Occupation Specialty) was 0311, Marine rifleman. Being a new replacement, I often found myself walking point at the front of our platoon, and I thought to myself, "They must have a lot of confidence in me if they'd let me walk out in front and lead the platoon." As I later came to realize, that wasn't the reason at all. "Out front" is where they always put the new guys, where you might contact the enemy first, so if you were going to be of any use to them at all, you'd have to do your "time in the bucket first."

But I did get a bit of a thrill walking point. Everyone moved at my pace; when I raised my hand and made a fist (a signal to instantly stop), everyone froze and waited to see what I did next. It made me feel like I was in control and leading the platoon. I was still young and full of that cockiness that can often lead to mistakes, and it's often those very mistakes that we have to survive before we gain real experience.

A Tragedy, Narrowly Averted

We were on a five-day sweep mission, just south and west of the city of Hue. During the day, we would sweep through the rice fields and into the jungles and thickets that surrounded the lowland hills. One afternoon, my platoon stopped to set up an ambush position. We were in a densely wooded spot on a hillside, just above a trail that led between two villages. Our intelligence reports said that this trail was being used by small bands of VC that would travel between the villages. We were hoping to catch some of them when they started moving at night time.

A platoon-size ambush was deployed by having the main group (1st, 2nd, and 3rd squads) position themselves parallel to, and away from the trail by about 15-30 meters. The Marines would either dig a temporary fighting holes, or position themselves securely behind some form of cover, so that they could easily view the trail and still be in a defensible position.

On either flank of the main body, "listening posts" (called LP's), consisting of two men (one carrying a radio), would find a concealed position alongside and back from the trail at approximately 50 yards ahead of or behind the main body. This way the LP's were able to give advance notice to the platoon when they saw someone on the trail. Once the main body was alerted, they would wait for their platoon commander's order to fire. All the squads are set up with interlocking fields of fire. It was a very deadly and effective tool.

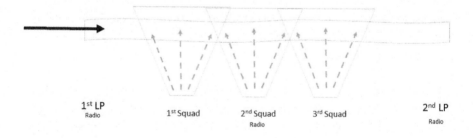

1st LP
Radio   1st Squad   2nd Squad   3rd Squad   2nd LP
                              Radio   Radio

I was assigned, along with another Marine (Lance Corporal Murray), to the LP on the right. Murray and I found a suitable position and settled in to wait out the rest of the afternoon. You never knew how long you'd be in one place, so it didn't pay to get too comfortable. By the same token, you could be there for many hours, so you had to be prepared for that as well.

Whenever we were on ambush duty, there was a strict code of
silence and it was absolutely essential that you stay alert, so one man
would rest for two hours, while the other one watched the trail and
also monitored the radio.

Every 20 or 30 minutes there would be a radio check[36] call from the
lieutenant or platoon sergeant. Because it was still daylight out,
L/Cpl. Murray decided to let me do the first two-hour watch as he
tried to get some rest.

It didn't take Murray long to go to sleep. He had a mild snoring
problem, and every now and then I'd nudge his shoulder a bit, and
he would stop for a while. The first hour had gone quietly. I'd
already completed two radio check-ins, when I suddenly heard a
loud noise, like a branch breaking.

My eyes immediately looked up at the trail, to a point where it
opened up out of a dense patch of trees. All my senses had kicked
into high gear, and I could feel the adrenaline rush. I quietly picked
up the radio handset with my right hand and my rifle with the other.
As I stared at that spot where the trees opened up, I saw a single
figure emerge, and then a second one behind him. They looked like
they were wearing black pajama bottoms and loose grey shirts. They
were both carrying rifles on their shoulders. I instantly called back to
the platoon commander to alert him.

"Mike-3, Mike-3, we have two - no, make that three bad guys on the
trail, and they're all carrying weapons!" The platoon commander
instantly came back, "Mike 3-3, Mike 3-3 (That was us, 3rd squad of
3rd platoon.), confirm you have three bad guys."

I was just about to answer when Murray woke up with a start, took
one look at the trail, and ripped the handset away from me. He yelled

---

[36] Radio checks – At the platoon level, whoever was carrying the radio for the platoon
commander would be responsible for making periodic calls to the other two radios to make
sure that all the radios were working properly, and that their operators were monitoring
the network.

(loud enough for the Vietnamese to hear), "Mike 3, Mike 3, they are not bad guys – REPEAT - they are not bad guys! They are farmers – REPEAT - they are farmers! OVER!"

I sat back in shock when I heard this, and as I was looked at the three Vietnamese on the trail, the weapons on their shoulders suddenly transformed into axes and saws. They were wood cutters, evidently coming back from clearing an area in the jungle to make it suitable for planting.

My mind had been so intent on looking for enemy soldiers that, in the excitement of the moment, what my brain registered as weapons, were in reality, just their normal wood cutting tools. If it hadn't been for Murray, they all would have been killed, and it would have been my fault. A mistake I would have to have lived with the rest of my life.

The shock of the tragedy that had almost happened was like being struck by a lightning bolt, and that shock stayed with me for several days after that. I just couldn't get it out of my mind that I had almost been responsible for three innocent men getting killed. To this day, when I think back on that moment, I silently thank the powers that be that Murray was there to correct that awful mistake.

But there was a positive thing that came out of that experience. After reviewing the incident in my mind so many times, I came to realize that I had succumbed to something akin to what we used to call back home "buck fever." Buck fever is what can sometimes happen to people who go hunting for the first time. It is the "nervous excitement of an inexperienced hunter upon the approach of game." I was the inexperienced hunter; so focused on relaying the message to the main ambush down the trail, that it was all I could see.

I vowed that would never happen to me again, and I started to change. I started noticing after that, when I would get into similar situations in the future, my mind would start to automatically shift to a small, emotionless, quiet spot before it made those kind of life and death decisions. In a way, that was good, because it served me well for the remainder of my tour in Vietnam. For me, there would be many more ambushes, and many more unique situations that I had never experienced before, or could even imagine. If you are a human being, there is no way to avoid having those feelings of fear, terror, or even sometimes, hopelessness, but if you can manage to set them aside, even for a few moments, then you've got an edge. And I think the experience of that near tragedy gave me an edge that helped me get through a lot of what I was going to have to face before I would get to go back home.

But, in another way, it wasn't so good, because that type of response stayed with me for a very long time after I had been out of the service. If someone close to me died, or I witnessed a tragic accident, in real time, my emotions would go cold until I could process the feelings later. Sometimes that was viewed as inappropriate by the people around me and I used to feel guilty and self-conscious about it, but it turns out that it's not an uncommon response among a lot of veterans that I've talked to.

[The following incident happened several weeks later, after we had moved our command center to Phu Bai, which was south of Camp Evans. I'm jumping ahead a bit here, but this story relates to the incident that I just talked about.

This event was recorded in our battalion command chronology, and also in a newspaper clipping, which I'll include here. I believe the newspaper article will add a little color to the story.]

I Don't Shoot Guys Wearing Suits!

It was March 16, 1967, about midday, and we had set up another ambush along a trail. The trail was being used by Viet Cong troops to go between villages, and also their own encampments in the hills.

This time I was not on one of the LP's, but rather, was in the main group of the ambush. We had been positioned there for a while when one of our LP's alerted us to the fact that we had a large group of VC moving down the trail.

As I readied myself, I could see the first man wearing black pajamas and carrying an AK-47, and then another, and another, until, right in the middle of the column, came a man wearing grey slacks, loafer style shoes, and a matching grey jacket with shirt and black tie. Additionally, he was carrying a small satchel with a strap that looked a bit like a camera bag. Next to him was a guy wearing a gray/green NVA uniform and a backpack. Even though I was much more seasoned now, I wasn't really ready for a guy who was wearing a *suit*.

The ambush was now set, and everyone was waiting for it to be triggered by the first shot from our lieutenant. I had to process the idea that I was going to have to shoot this guy. Then, everything seemed to happen at once when the lieutenant fired his weapon. We all opened up at the same time, and I remember my mind silently shouting, "I don't shoot guys in suits!" And I didn't. I shot the first guy in front of him, skipped the "suit guy" in the middle, and fired several rounds at the next guy, who was also carrying an AK-47. Evidently, no one else in the platoon had any problems whatsoever with shooting the "suit guy", because he went down almost immediately. Then a surprising thing happened.

The bag that "suit guy" was carrying had been hit by several rounds of automatic weapons fire, and it exploded into a showering cascade of money that drifted slowly to the ground, all along the trail.

I don't know how much money was there, but it sure seemed to be a lot. It was a very colorful sight to see, because all the Vietnamese money was in small paper bills, which came in all different colors. It was like a rainbow had exploded.

It took a little while for all that money to finally come to rest, and then when it did, it was all over the place. It took a while, but we finally got the ambush site secured. The money was picked up, enemy weapons and gear secured, and then the incident was reported back to our battalion headquarters.

Just one more thing to do. Our platoon commander, Lt. Manzi, walked to the front of the platoon and yelled, "OK, everybody, turn in the rest of the damn money!" No one moved; they all just stood around with innocent looks on their faces, and shuffled their feet. The lieutenant rolled his eyes, shook his head and directed all the squad leaders to "shake down the men." (After all these years, I still laugh, every time I think about it.)

Eventually, almost all of the money was collected, except for a few souvenir notes that people just refused to give up. While looking through enemy packs for any intelligence documents, it was discovered that the VC had also been carrying 25 lbs. of "rock candy", most likely for their field troops (even the enemy has a sweet tooth). None of the candy would ever make it to its intended destination in the field, or, for that matter, would even find its way back to our battalion headquarters. Our squad leaders had already divided it up for their men, and they weren't giving the candy back either. It seemed only fair to me.

(See next page for article from the III MAF Newspaper, "The Sea Tiger")

Sweet tooth Viet Cong

PHU BAI—The Viet Cong have a sweet tooth, too.

Incuded in the possessions of one of four VC killed by a platoon of "M" Company, Twenty-Sixth Marines, was about 25 pounds of assorted hard candy.

"I guess we must have caught the enemy on a candy run," said Private First Class Robert D. Wetzel, who serves as a sniper.

The platoon killed two VC during one early morning ambush and accounted for two more in a similar ambush a day later while operating in the Co Bi Thanh Tan valley, 25 miles northwest of Hue.

"One of the VC was a paymaster. He was carrying his records with him," Second Lieutenant John D. Manzi, the platoon commander said. "We also captured some food supplies and clothing in addition to the candy," he said.

Manzi said three Viet Cong walked into the first ambush, but apparently began to suspect something just before they reached the kill zone. Only one escaped into the brush, however.

Chapter 7

Phu Bai Combat Base

We were still at Camp Evans and had been in the field for about ten days. When we returned, the entire battalion was ordered to move by truck convoy to Phu Bai, which would be our new area of operations and command center for the next few months. It was like leaving an old frontier town and moving to the big city.

Instead of tents, bunkers, and water filled fighting holes, we now would have actual barracks with elevated floors, screen siding, and a tin roof over our heads. And every building was surrounded by a sandbagged wall. Inside, we each had a cot to sleep on, and for the first time since being in-country, I didn't feel like I was going to die from hypothermia during the night, or get carried off by mosquitos.

Dear Mom,   3-11-1967

We're at Phu Bai now, and just taking it easy. We're on "Sparrow Hawk" duty, which is like garrison standby, in case anyone in the field gets in trouble, but it gives us a lot of time to rest up.

We had breakfast this morning at their mess hall and it was outstanding. We had hot cakes and syrup, fresh fried eggs, fried potatoes, bacon, dry cereal with real milk, fresh bread and jam, orange juice and coffee. They tell me that's a pretty routine breakfast around here so I think I'm going to like this place. We used to get an occasional hot meal at Camp Evans but since we spent most of our time in the field . I've been eating a lot of C-Rations up until now

Oh, almost forgot to tell you, they even have movies here sometimes and a small PX so I'll tell you more about that when I get a chance to see them.

[This is a picture with Francis Tydingo (nicknamed "Tiger"). He and I went through boot camp and ITR training together back at Camp Pendleton. Tiger and I also shipped out together to Vietnam, and were both assigned to Mike Company's 3rd Platoon. That's our barracks in the background. Tiger was originally from Guam.]

[A picture of the barracks at Phu Bai. This was like heaven after Camp Evans.]

The next two days were spent doing "Rough Rider" duty, which is providing security for truck convoys running up Hwy 1 from Phu Bai to Camp Evans, and then back in the evening.

Once we would get back to Phu Bai, we would be on "Sparrow Hawk" duty, which meant we were on a 15-minute standby status as a reactionary force, should anyone need help out in the field. This meant we were supposed to get hot meals in the morning and evening, but that turned out to be short-lived. The next eight days found us out in the field again, running more sweeps and ambushes at night. The nighttime activity between the villages, and the more frequent assaults on our CAC units (Combined Action Companies) meant that the VC activities and troop concentrations were increasing.

We would spend the next three months headquartered at Phu Bai. The routine became a blur of 2-3 days inside the camp doing Rough Rider and Sparrow Hawk duties, then we would spend 6-8 days out in the field running sweeps and night time ambushes.

I have a number of specific memories for that period, but it was very difficult to tie those memories in with an exact time or place. One resource that I had for recounting events was the 3rd Battalion, 26th Regiment's Command Chronology.[37]The Chronology is simply a day-to-day, sometimes hour-by-hour, log of significant activity notes that were turned in each day by the platoon and company commanders. In most cases, they are sparse on details, but they do carry times, map locations, and a very spare accounting of our daily activities. Sometimes the notes are no more than an estimated count of VC we had encountered, how many confirmed kills, and our own count of KIAs and WIAs, as well as an inventory of enemy weapons of an inventory of enemy weapons that were captured.

I rarely, if ever, wrote to Mom about what happened out in the field. It would just worry her, and I'm sure there was a lot she would never

---

[37] http://www.khesanh.org/chronology/26thmarines/3rdbn/index.html

understand, so I always tried to keep things light and informal when I wrote to her.

During the spring and early summer of 1967, we were very successful with the strategies of deploying an ambush. Our company turned this strategy almost into an art form. We took our share of casualties, but we inflicted many times more. Battalion and Regimental Headquarters seemed to
gauge our success solely on 'body counts', and they even turned it into a contest between the various companies, providing 'beer parties' at the end of each month for whichever company tallied up the most. It seemed like my company (Mike Company) was always winning that contest.

Landmine Warfare School

Around mid-March I was chosen, along with other squad leaders and NCOs, to attend a three-day "Landmine Warfare School." I remember Sgt. Holley and several others from our platoon also attending. There were representatives of all the other platoons and companies in our battalion. Each class consisted of about 25 students, and there were three instructors who gave classroom lectures. There were field exercises as well (That means we got to blow things up). One of our instructors was a Chu Hoi (Which means a "Defector"). He was an ex-Viet Cong, and he had been trained in the North on how to design and deploy explosives. When he defected to the South, he was quickly picked up as a consultant to the 3rd Marine Division's initiative to have classes that trained Marines for what to look for out in the field.

The other two instructors were USMC engineers, and they focused on the types of explosives that we would use in field operations for clearing away trees, bunkers, and other obstacles. Often, we would use explosives to safely detonate and dispose of booby traps and unexploded bombs in the field. I was surprised that there was actually a lot of math involved, but most of our attention was fixed on how to handle the explosives that we would be working with.

All three instructors were very good at keeping our attention, and no one fell asleep during their classes. Many times they would start a session by holding up an explosive, or explosive device, and stating, "Now this little beauty, if it was to go off, will easily kill everyone in the room."

I made a mental note to not sit in the front row after that, but I don't think that would have mattered very much. I also remember our first session on C-4 explosives. The instructor held up a small brick of C-4, with the customary cautionary note that "it could kill everyone in the room." he proceeded to take his knife and shave off a chunk of it. He then laid it back on his desk and lit it on fire with his lighter. It immediately burst into an intense, white flame, and continued to blaze while he went on with the classroom instruction.

He said, "As you can see, C-4 is quite safe to work with. You can even light it on fire. You would need 2500 pounds of it, burning in a large pile, before it would explode. But," he added, "with the use of a small detonating cap," as he pulled one out of his pocket and pushed it into the brick.

There was a long pause, as he just stared at us, waiting for a response. That's when the whole class shouted together, "IT WILL KILL EVERYONE IN THE F*CKING ROOM!" Our instructor seemed quite pleased that we had been paying attention.

Later we had a session from the Vietnamese Chu Hoi, and although his English was broken, and we had a little trouble understanding him, he was just as entertaining. On the desk in front of him he had a collection of cans and boxes. He started out, "You Americans, you love to kick can; you love to kick box; anything you see on the road, you kick it! Why that? We[38] don't know; we just know you like to kick it!"

---

[38] The "We" he was referring to was when he used to be a Viet Cong.

Then, to illustrate his point, he picked up one of the cans on the desk and turned it upside down. Out dropped a grenade, and the safety pin popped off and both bounced around on the floor. Everyone in the class tried to dive under their desks at the same time.

When the grenade didn't go off, we nervously climbed back in our seats. All the instructors were still standing there, motionless, with deadpan faces. Then the Chu Hoi instructor reached over, picked up a box, turned it upside down, and out popped three more grenades, with the pins all popping as they bounced onto his desk and onto the floor.

Once again, we all tried to jump for cover. You'd have thought by now we would have seen it coming, but the mere sight of three (potentially live) grenades bouncing all over the place was just too much for our brains to ignore. My platoon had already encountered similar booby traps at least six times, and we'd lost several Marines and had an additional half dozen casualties. He probably could have gone on doing the same demonstration over and over and we'd still be jumping out of our seats, but instead, he finished up the session with the simple admonition, "Don't kick cans, don't kick boxes!"

The final two days of class were more technical in nature as we learned, for instance, the differences between "time fuses" and "detonation cords." One of the first things I noticed was that they looked very similar, but they were very different in how they were used. "Time cord" would burn at about 3 feet per minute, and "detonation cord" burned at about 22,000 feet per second.

Detonation cord is actually an explosive, and could be used to wrap around trees, or similarly odd shaped objects, and then they could be blown in place by attaching a "time fuse" with a blasting cap to the detonation cord. This was similar to the way we would detonate C-4 explosive.

Probably the most interesting demonstration that I witnessed though was when the instructor took six grenades, unscrewed the levers and removed the blasting caps, leaving just the main part of the grenade. Then he took a long length of detonation cord, and for every 10 ft., he would make a small loop in the cord and place it inside the cavity of one of the disassembled grenades.

He continued on in this way with three more grenades, all spaced about 10 feet apart. To the end of the detonation cord he attached about 6 feet of time fuse. We were all watching from the safety of a bunker as the time fuse slowly burned and eventually reached the cord. Everything along the 40foot string exploded at once, detonation cord, grenades, shrapnel flying everywhere; it was one humongous and deadly explosion.

We got further instruction on how to look for booby traps, and especially trip wires. Obviously, you want to watch where you're stepping but the Viet Cong had different ways of letting their brethren know that an area was booby trapped, such as odd rock or stick arrangements along the trail. There was no one single guide to how these would be marked, you just had to be aware and careful.

During the remainder of my time in Vietnam, I never had an opportunity to use my newly found knowledge of explosives except in one instance. From time to time, we would be able to acquire a small amount of C-4 from some of the engineers. C-4 was quite safe to carry in your pocket, and quite handy to have when you wanted to slice off a very small chuck, light it on fire, and brew a cup of coffee in about 20 seconds.

I Get Promoted to Fire Team Leader

It wasn't long after I returned from the Landmine Warfare School that I was told that I was being made a temporary fire team leader. I had now been in-country for several months and by most standards was considered a veteran.

We had a new batch of replacements come in from the States, and I was asked to step up and be a fire team leader, because one of the corporals in our platoon had broken an ankle and was no longer with the platoon.

In the Marines Corps, a fire team was composed of 4 men, which included the fire team leader and 3 additional riflemen. There were 3 fire teams in a squad, and 3 squads in a platoon. With the addition of a platoon commander (a lieutenant), that should total around 37 men, but with losses, and people in coming and going, it was more likely to be 30-32 men in a platoon at any given time.

I had never had any formal leadership training. In fact, the new NCO schools[39], which included leadership training, wouldn't be instituted by the Marine Corps for another six months. In any case, being a PFC, I wouldn't have qualified to go to one of those schools anyway, I would have to wait until I advanced one more level to lance/corporal before I could be considered for that.

As it turned out, I would only be a fire team leader for a few weeks, until we received more NCO's from one of the other Marine battalions. Still, I was very happy to have this opportunity, and I wanted to make the best of it while I could.

My Fire Team

Not a very good picture, but these are the three young Marines on my fire team. I wish I could remember everyone's name, but after so many years, the only one I remember is Edgar Wayne Thompson, who is posing here with his rifle. If you had ever known Wayne, you would probably never forget him. One of the most personable young men I had ever met or been around. If you go to look up the words "exuberance and confidence" in the dictionary, there should be a picture of Wayne there.

---

[39] NCO stands for non-commissioned officers, and this refers to the ranks of E-4 (Corporal) or higher, all the way up to E-9, which can be the ranks of 1st Sergeant or Master Sergeant.

[PFC Edgar Thompson, who is holding the rifle, and the other 2 Marines on the left were members of my fire team.]

In this particular photograph, we were out in the field in company strength, and we had set up a large perimeter. We were going to wait here for a resupply helicopter that was scheduled for the next morning. Wayne decided it was a good time for a photo op, so he grabbed his rifle and struck a menacing pose. As I grabbed my camera, he shouted out, "Have you ever seen a Marine as bad-ass as me?"

I was looking at Wayne, trying to assess his total level of "bad ass-ness," and I said, "That's pretty bad looking, Thompson, but I still think Smitty is looking just a little bit badder than you." Wayne looked at Smitty (on his right in the picture), and with the cigarette still dangling out of his mouth, he said, "Don't worry, we'll cut him out of the picture later."

And he was true to his word. When I finally got the pictures back, I gave one copy to Wayne, and he immediately cut everyone else out of the picture. Wayne said he was going to send it home to have a Christmas card made up out of it.

After hearing that I was from Iowa, one of the other guys in my fire team said that he had a girlfriend who had been a senior last year (1966) at Lane Tech High School in Des Moines. I wondered if my brother Richard knew her, because he had been a senior at Lane Tech that same year. Before I thought to ask his girlfriend's name, we had changed the subject.

(Years later, I happened to see a 1966 Lane Tech High School yearbook at one of their class reunions that I attended with a friend. I remembered the incident from way back in my Vietnam days, but had forgotten the young Marine's name. Try as I might, I couldn't dredge it up from my brain, and it left me with a sad feeling of regret because I would have had an opportunity to see if he, the young Marine in my fire team, had survived to return home.)

We Get Ambushed

Although we had been very successful with our nighttime ambushes, sometimes the VC could give as good as they got.

We were working just south of Phu Bai in the Phu Loc district. According to the Command Chronology records, it was around 1930 hours (7:30 PM), and we were on a narrow jungle trail, heading for the map coordinates where we were supposed to be setting up our ambush.

I was no longer a fire team leader; I had been replaced when the new NCOs arrived, and I was now back in my former duty as a rifleman. But this night I was also carrying the 2nd squad's radio. This wasn't the first (or last) time I would carry a radio. Each platoon had three radios. As far as I can recall, we didn't have any trained radiomen left, so riflemen were picked at random to carry them. Each of the three squads needed a radio and they were utilized by the platoon commander and two of the squad leaders.

Tonight it was my turn to carry the radio, a PRC-25 that weighed about 30 lbs. with its spare battery. With my regular pack, which was strapped over and around the radio, it was pretty bulky as well, but at 6 feet tall and 190 lbs., I was a little bigger than most of the guys, so I was getting picked more often to carry one. As it turned out, that was very fortunate for me.

We had been walking down a trail when, suddenly, we started receiving automatic weapons fire from about 15-20 yards away on our right. There was a long, narrow ditch on the left of the trail, and we all dove for that. I landed on my feet, but the weight of the pack, and radio flung me on my back against the opposite side of the ditch. As I fell hard against the back wall of the ditch, I could feel (and hear) a snapping, crunching sound, and then I felt a sharp pain in my lower back along the right side.

I tried to pull away, and immediately realized that we were also in the middle of a patch of barbed wire that was strung throughout the length of the ditch. It was almost impossible to get into a firing position because, when I'd try to straighten up, the barb wire would cut into my arms and chest and pull me back down.

As I worked at trying to untangle myself from the wire, my platoon had started returning fire - with a vengeance. We estimated that they (the VC) had fired about 25 rounds, point blank at us, and we had returned several times that amount in return. We found two dead VC, and blood trails where the others had gotten away. Our point man had been killed outright, and 11 more Marines in my platoon were pretty torn up by the barbed wire.

When it was all over, and the area was secured, we were able to extricate ourselves from the wire. This took a while, and as the adrenaline rush started to subside, that's when I noticed that, besides the cuts from the barbed wire, I had a bleeding gash, and a sharp pain in my lower back.

I was the only one who had been thrown against the back wall of the Ditch. Along its walls were rows of old, brittle punji sticks. That was what I had felt crunching and breaking against my back pack and radio. Two sticks had hit the radio directly, and a third one made its way into my back. Fortunately for me, it only penetrated about an inch, instead of impaling me, as it would have if I had not been carrying the pack and radio.

The next morning, we were back in Phu Bai, and I got treatment for all the lacerations from the barb wire, but what was most worrisome was the wound from the punji stick. I was treated with heavy doses of antibiotics and watched closely for the next several days. Thankfully I didn't develop a serious infection, and after several days, I was put back on the active duty roster. Ironically, the next time out in the field, I'd catch a bug that sent me back to sick bay for seven days, and it was even more serious; it could have killed me. And it all came from drinking the water.

Bad Water

When we would go out into the field or jungle, water was critical, but you can only carry so much. Typically, I'd carry two to three canteens. Sometimes that would barely last a day or two, so it was vitally important to have a water supply available. For the most part, we would get that from rivers and streams. If none were available (and that was rare), we would have to be resupplied by helicopter, but that would only be in emergencies.

Almost all the water that was available to us was unsafe to drink for one reason or another. Treating it with Halizone[40] tablets was mandatory. We were told that Halizone tablets were very effective in killing all the bad bugs that were floating around, but the truth was somewhat different, because Halizone, by itself, was less effective in tropical climates. Halizone made the water smell even worse, and you needed to wait 10-15 minutes before drinking it.

Here's what happened to me. Several weeks after my barbed wire and punji stick episode, we were again in the field, and on the second day, I stopped at a stream to refill my canteens. I actually have a picture of this, because I asked one of our guys, PFC Gomez,

---

[40] Halizone tablets were the pills that we were given for water purification.

to snap my picture. We'd been following an old road that ran parallel to a stream, and we were taking a break. I dropped my pack and radio and climbed down the bank to the stream.

I was the only one who took water from that stream. That evening I started to get really sick with diarrhea and eventually dehydration. It was another two days before we came back out of the field, and all I remember, once we got back to Phu Bai, was making my way towards the sick bay tent.

[That is me in the lower left, filling my canteens from that slow moving stream. I remembered to add Halizone tablets to my canteens, but it did not kill all the bugs in the water.]

I spent the next seven days in sick bay, and don't remember anything about it. Even after I was well enough to get back to the platoon, I still had no memories of those days. Sgt. Holley and Lt. Manzi both checked in on me when I was in sick bay, but I was hooked up to fluids, and in and out of consciousness, and don't remember seeing them.

Long Day's Journey into Night

It took me another full week before I started feeling normal again. Luckily, we were still on Sparrow Hawk and Road Runner duty, so I was able to spend most of that time in our comfortable barracks in Phu Bai. But that was not to last much longer. We again received the word to "get ready." We were going back out in the field for another 5-7 days running daytime sweeps and night time ambushes.

One day, Mike-3 (the 3rd platoon) had broken from its normal routine[41], and we were forced to hike all day and into the late afternoon over rugged rolling hills. The hills would abruptly drop down steep embankments into sunken valleys. It was some of the densest jungle that we had yet encountered. The going was painfully slow.

I was now part of a four-man fire team, often walking the point of the column. Whomever was walking as our lead man had to literally cut his way through overgrown vegetation and bamboo thickets. The heavy growth looked as if it had never seen the touch of a human being before. Our point man would hack through the vegetation with a machete, sometimes only moving a few yards a minute. The physical drain, in the high heat and high humidity, would eventually take its toll on the lead man, and necessitate that another man takes his place, until, the replacement would have to be replaced himself.

This day the job of 'cutting trail' fell upon our two men walking point, Eriksson and Halsey. They traded off places in this fashion all afternoon until the heat and effort became almost too much. I could tell they were starting to lose it. At one point, Halsey, who had been hacking away at a particularly stubborn patch of branches and bamboo, finally threw down his machete, backed up about 20 feet and went barreling head-on, throwing the entire weight of his body

---

[41] Our normal routine when conducting night time ambushes was to move to a new location during the day, set up in what was called a "rabbit position," which was basically a secure perimeter, and every other man would be allowed to get some sleep while the other was on guard. Just after dark, we would slip out, hopefully unnoticed, to a nighttime ambush position. This particular day, we broke routine by marching all day.

onto the nearly impenetrable wall of vegetation. Then, he rebounded back like he had just run in to a rubber wall.

Eriksson, rolling his eyes and shaking his head, stepped over Halsey, picked up the machete, and slowly started hacking away at the underbrush. Halsey quietly got up and took his place behind Eriksson, saving his strength because he knew his turn would come again soon enough. Never once did I hear either of them curse or complain.

I had been assigned to carry a radio (again) along with my normal pack and gear. The extra 30 lbs. made it more difficult to walk, but mercifully spared me from having to share the responsibility of swinging the machete and blazing trail. I'm sure that either Eriksson or Halsey would have traded places with me in a heartbeat.

It seemed like we had been walking forever, and as the late afternoon began to turn into twilight, we were approaching the map coordinates where the Lieutenant wanted to set us up.

Mercifully, we finally came across the semblance of a trail. We followed it for another half hour, when the lieutenant called the platoon to a halt. It was completely dark by now, and extremely difficult see our surroundings in the moonless night.

The main part of the ambush was set up on the north side of the trail and parallel to it. The lieutenant sent out listening posts to position themselves about 50 yards ahead and behind of where the platoon was set in to give an advance notice if someone approached from either end. I was assigned, along with Cpl. Halsey, to be part of the forward listening post.

As Halsey and I made our way down the trail, looking for a likely setup position, the vegetation and overgrowth on our right became so thick that, if we were to venture too far into it, we might not be able to see the trail at all. So, after we had gone about 50 yards, we decided to start looking on the left side. There we found it to be a little more favorable, with a number of low lying bushes to help hide our position, but still giving us a view to the trail. We just needed to find a good spot.

As we made our way off the trail, we found a location that seemed to be ideal, about 40-50 feet from the trail itself, and with enough cover (we thought at the time) to provide us with sufficient concealment. As we would later find out, in our haste to find a good location for the listening post and to finally be able to settle down and rest from the exhausting exertions of the day, we had made several mistakes in judgment that we would later have to deal with.

Good Morning Vietnam!

The protocol for a two-man, nighttime position was that either Halsey or I would take turns sleeping, while the other stayed awake. The awake man would watch the trail and also monitor the radio.

Sometime during the night, the unthinkable happened. We *both* fell asleep at the same time. That had never happened before, and it never happened after, but it did happen that night. To this day, I can't remember who was supposed to be standing watch. I don't think it really mattered. After all those exhausting hours of cutting trail, or in my case, of humping a radio, both Halsey and I were doomed from the beginning to crash in the cool darkness of that quiet jungle evening.

It was near daybreak when I was awakened by Halsey, lightly tapping me on the arm. I was lying flat on my back with my feet pointed in the direction of the trail. Halsey was on his back, but pointing in the opposite direction. His head was contorted back and downwards; he was peering at the trail while still maintaining that bizarre position.

I heard a quiet and low sounding, "Shush!" come from Halsey. I raised my head slightly and looked in the direction of the trail. The very first thing I noticed was that the bush we had chosen to hide behind was not very good cover at all. What had seemed to be a solid covering of leaves and branches in the dark now looked more like a $10 Christmas tree, the kind that are always the last to be sold because they're so anemic looking.

The next thing I noticed, as I peered directly through the semi-bare branches of the bush, was that there were two men on the trail, dressed in black pajamas and carrying automatic weapons. Both were leaning towards us and staring directly at our" hiding spot." They seemed confused. Then they started talking to each other, as if they were trying to decide exactly what it was that they were looking at. Unfortunately, our anemic little bush wasn't sufficient cover to completely save us from at least, catching their attention.

Without moving a muscle, I let my eyes look over to my right to see where my rifle was and also to see what Halsey's situation was. He was doing the exact same thing and was giving me this solid, piercing stare. After all these years I can still see that stare of his, and I remember that there was absolutely no fear in his eyes. There was no room for fear, because now, the only way we had to communicate with each other was with our eyes. It was our only means of communication, any quick movement on our part would have given us away. In order to reach our rifles, we would need to first pick them up, and then raise ourselves into a firing position. By then, we would most likely be dead. It would be like being in an old western quick draw contest and telling your opponent, "You go first."

My arms were at my side, and as all these thoughts were racing through my head, I started feeling around with my hands. That's when I remembered that in my right pocket, I carried a hand grenade. I never did like using the grenade pouches they issued, so I just always kept one in my right pants pocket, where the pin would be protected from accidently catching on something. I reached in and slowly worked my hand around the grenade, and even more slowly removed it from my pocket and inched it up to a resting position on my chest.

I wasn't 100% sure that this was going to be our best strategy, so I redirected my attention back to Halsey's eyes. At this point, I think we had achieved an almost perfect psychic connection with each other, and I could see his head move ever so slightly up and down in agreement. There even seemed to be the tinniest bit of a glimmer in his eyes, as if to say, "Go for it!"

So, now we had a plan. As I got ready to pull the pin and throw it, I realized there was going to be another problem. Because of the weight of a grenade, it can't be thrown like a baseball, and the effective kill radius, about 15 meters, meant that I was going to have to get it out at least to the trail, which was 40-50 feet away. If I tried to pull the pin, raise up and then turn my body in order to throw the grenade overhand, we were going to be in the same situation (or worse) than if we tried to use our rifles. Our plan was that the sight of a live grenade, flying out from a bush, would startle them just long enough to give us an edge in the firefight that was about to happen.

I decided that the only way this would work would be if I quietly pulled the pin while the grenade was still on my chest, then let go of the pin while trying to execute something like a pitch to halfback in football. I'd have to lob it forward from my chest, as hard as I could, and just hope that it traveled far enough away so that we wouldn't be its unintended victims.

There wasn't any time to try to communicate all this to Halsey. Any second now, the two enemy scouts (turns out they were part of a larger patrol) would be walking over to check out our bush, so I pulled the pin, and in one fast movement, lobbed the grenade out as high and hard as I could. At the same time, Halsey and I both went for our weapons. Just as we grabbed our weapons and got into a sitting position to fire, the grenade went off. Despite that forceful heave I had given it, it must not have made it all the way to the trail, and we ducked as the explosion sent shrapnel whizzing over our heads.

Caught in the Middle.

The sound of the grenade exploding triggered the ambush. Everyone in our 3rd platoon started firing all at once (from directly behind us). The two VC scouts and their buddies began returning fire. Bullets were now buzzing at us - from both directions! Our platoon - and the VC - were both shooting at *us*!

It seems we'd made another critical mistake the previous evening, in our search for a good hiding spot. We had failed to notice that the trail itself was making a gentle, but definite turn to our left, so the place that we had ended up finally choosing was in *the direct line of fire of our own people.*

We didn't even try to get into the fight. We just hugged the ground until finally, thankfully, after several minutes, the shooting stopped. The enemy patrol had high-tailed it, and our guys now came running up and shouting to us, "What happened?" What happened?" We didn't know what to say to them, so we ended up just not saying anything at all.

There was a blood trail (one or both of the VC scouts had been wounded by the grenade), so our platoon spent the next half hour trying to chase them down. Eventually, it was time for us to move out to find a new position for the next ambush and the whole question of "who threw that first grenade" was thankfully forgotten.

I Am Promoted to Platoon Radioman

It was just a few days after this last incident that Lt. Manzi asked me if I wanted to be his radioman. I wasn't used to being "asked" to do anything in the Marines. I immediately said "Yes, I'd like that very much." Although carrying and managing the radio every day meant it was going to be tougher out in the field carrying the extra weight, I liked the idea of knowing right away when the lieutenant gave orders to his squad leaders. It also meant I was likely to get a promotion sooner than later if I did a good job.

One of the first things I asked the lieutenant was, "Would I ever be required to call in mortar or artillery fire?" I had never been formally

[**Bill Halsey** and **George Eriksson** in the upper left. They had both been with the Battalion since it was first reactivated. That's me, lower right. We referred to anyone who had been with the Battalion since the beginning as "Originals." (Picture courtesy of Sgt. Rhett Holley.)]

trained in combat communications or tactical map reading, and both were required knowledge for calling in artillery.

Reading a tactical map is totally different that reading a road map. It's basically a topographical map with its own set of coordinates, and we used a variety of different maps almost every time we moved into a new area. The Lieutenant assured me that only he, or the platoon sergeant, or squad leaders would be doing that[42]. However, there was one thing he did want me to learn, and I was going to need to spend some time practicing it.

Counting Steps

When out in the field, one of the most difficult logistical problems is

---

[42] As it would turn out, not technically true, because in the coming weeks, I would have an opportunity to "call in artillery fire".

knowing exactly where you are at any given time. If you're moving in the open, or if there are landmarks that you can see, it's much easier to pinpoint your location on the map. Many times, however, we would be moving through dense jungle with double or triple canopy overhead. At times like that, even getting the position of the sun might be impossible. Navigating at night only adds to the difficulty.

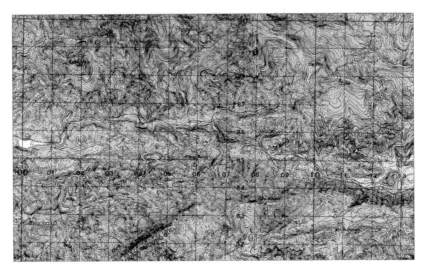

[This is what a tactical map looks like. There are rarely, if ever, any roads, buildings or landmarks. There are, however, rivers, streams, and elevation changes, and a grid work of coordinates that are used to help call in artillery and mortar fire.]

Infantry officers get quite a bit of training with a compass and maps, and they are even taught little tricks, like having their radioman count their steps, and then periodically, taking a map reading to stay on course. That works fine in an open field where the radioman can take measured steps in a straight line, but in the jungle, with all the twisting, turning, slippery muddy ground underfoot, and the elevation changes, it's nearly impossible to take a "measured step."

To get me started, Lt. Manzi took me out to the open area in front of the barracks. He gave me a starting point and a destination about 100 yards away. Before I started off marching to the designated point in the distance, I asked him how long a step I should take, and he replied, "Just take your normal step and then count them as you go. Then turn around and count your steps back. Then let me know what the two numbers are."

At first I was afraid it was a test of some kind, and I was nervous. I was afraid I was going to fail, but when I got back to where he was standing, I reported that I'd taken 134 steps out and 129 steps back. That didn't seem too good to me, but the lieutenant said that was fine. Then he told me to repeat this same drill four more times. "Just take your time, remember to take your normal steps, write down the numbers, and bring them back to me" he said. I spent the next hour marching back and forth, writing down the numbers, and slowly it dawned on me what he was doing; he was calibrating my counts to the actual distance. They all seemed to be within +/- 6 or steps, so, if I walked 130 steps, then I'd traveled pretty close to 100 yards.

By the same reasoning, for every 100 steps I'd take, I would travel approximately 77 yards (give or take). It's more likely he was doing his calibrations in meters, because that's how the maps were laid out. It would be a simple mental calculation for him to ask me what the count was, and if I'd say something like 887 steps, he could round that to 900, and then do the math in his head. The trick was that all the little rounding errors and step variances would tend to cancel each other out, and he would end up with a fairly accurate assessment.

Pretty good for traveling along a jungle trail in absolute darkness, I thought. Except there was still the problem of it being impossible to take a measured step when we were trekking along broken paths in the dark. I was going to mention my concern the next day but by then he had a new drill for me to practice.

The next morning, Lt. Manzi said, "Now we're going to try something a little different. I want you to count your normal steps, but start taking some side steps and stutter steps, and some diagonal steps. Mix it up, but count the regular steps and then, when you can't take a regular forward step, don't count until you think you've moved forward a full step."

This was a lot harder, and at first I didn't understand what he was talking about, so he showed me how he wanted it done. I was sure now that I was going to flunk this part of the training, but I went ahead and practiced that on my own for the rest of the morning. I used the same 100-yard path I'd taken the day before.

I was sure that I looked ridiculous out there; marching around all morning long in broken lines, back and forth, all by myself. I was waiting for some sergeant to come out and ask me "what the hell" I was doing, but no one ever said anything, and everyone pretty much left me alone.

I wasn't very happy with the numbers I was coming up with. Before, they were fairly consistent, but not now, and a few times I even lost count, because I was thinking about all the pairs of eyes that were watching, wondering if I was crazy. After a while I started to wonder if this was some type of punishment, but if it was, I couldn't figure out what it might be.

The next morning, I reported to the lieutenant, and gave him the slip of paper with the numbers on it. I thought he was going to be upset because they weren't very consistent and much, much worse than when I was just marching straight ahead. But the lieutenant didn't seem to mind. Then he said something that totally confused me.

"Ward, if you need to go somewhere, or do something, just remember where you were and what your count was, then go back to the same place and continue. If you want to sit down somewhere and take a break, go ahead, just remember your count and where you were."

I went out to the open area and started again, but by now I was convinced that this must be some kind of mental test, or I actually was being punished. It just made no sense at all to me. I finished practicing in the morning, then went to the chow hall, and took my time coming back. I did another two hours or so that afternoon, took a few breaks, went back to the barracks, and talked to some of the guys (By now most of them were aware of what I was doing, but no one asked the lieutenant about it.)

By the third day it had just become routine, and counting the steps was just an afterthought. I realized that I could think about other things, and the count was still going on in the back of my head. It didn't really seem to matter anymore, because he never said anything to me about the numbers; he'd just look at them and then put them away.

I was starting to notice something. The numbers were beginning to get more consistent. It was starting to get to the point where I could march all over that practice area, even turning around and going backwards (just for a change), do some stutter steps, oblique steps, sideways steps, and by the time I got to the other end, some of the counts were even coming out the same.

It finally dawned on me that he was turning me into an odometer, only a human hybrid odometer who only counted forward motion. My brain was logging fairly accurate distances, even when traveling over broken jungle trails at night. I was starting to get pretty excited about this, because, as far as I knew, no one had ever tried doing this before.

I remember once asking one of the real radiomen in the communications center about it, and he said, "Oh sure, we all can do that," but then when I questioned him some more, I realized he didn't have the vaguest idea of what I was talking about. He was thinking, "Oh, counting steps - big deal."

When we next went out in the field, the first thing I asked the lieutenant was, "Do I start counting now?" He was busy with something, and turned around with an annoyed look and snapped back at me, "Ward, I'll tell you when to start counting," and then went back to what he was doing. The lieutenant rarely took the time to explain anything to me, or anyone else for that matter, but that wasn't unusual. He was the same way with all his squad leaders, and that was because he trusted them to carry out his orders. They didn't need explanations. Now he was treating me that way. I liked that.

We'd been walking along a small path next to a tree line for about half an hour when we turned away from the flat ground and started making our way into the denser wooded area. The lieutenant turned to me and said, "Start counting," and I did.

At first it was taking up all my attention as I tried to concentrate on taking regular-sized steps. Sometimes I'd get a little confused when we'd start to drift off of our original "straight direction path," and I found myself paying more attention to the counting than I was to where I was stepping, or what was happening around me. So I decided to just keep counting and not worry about how accurate it was going to end up being. If we'd been walking for a while off the original line, I'd just subtract a small number from the count. But for the most part I had little confidence that my numbers were going to do the lieutenant much good.

It was just starting to get dark when we finally reached a small stream, and the lieutenant stopped the column and asked for the count. After consulting the map, he turned the column left, and we followed it downstream for about 100 yards until we had reached a place where the stream forked. Here we stopped and set up our night time ambush position about 30 yards back from the edge of the stream.

The Lieutenant then grabbed the radio handset and tried to get ahold of Mike Company's 2nd platoon, "Mike-2, Mike-2, this is Mike-3, over." He tried two more times with no luck, then he said, "Damn! We're right on time, and right where we're supposed to be, and they're still lost somewhere on their side of the hill." Every 15 minutes, I would try to raise Mike 2, and after about an hour, we finally made contact. Mike 2 had just reached their position (a blocking position about 1 klick[43] away along a path that led down the right fork of the stream).

Later that night, as I was sitting up, watching the trail along the stream on my two hour rotation, I kept replaying the lieutenant's words through my mind, *"We're right on time, and right where we're supposed to be"*

I never did ask the lieutenant how I did, and he never said anything about it, but from then on, he and I used that technique a lot, especially when we were travelling through jungle or forested areas for long distances. It just became second nature for me to keep a running count in my head whenever he told me "start counting."[44]

Some Downtime at Phu Bai

I'd been in-country about three months now, and was starting feel pretty comfortable with my unit, and in my new role as a radioman. I had a lot of respect for the "old salts" in the unit, and I was getting to know some of the newer replacements that were coming into the platoon, but that's not to say that I knew everyone really well. You don't get a lot of time when you're in the field to chit-chat, so, aside from talking with the people in my fire team or squad, the only time to socialize was when we were back at Phu Bai while on stand down or Sparrow Hawk status. Usually this meant a lot of idle time spent around the barracks or visiting the small PX that had been established there.

---

[43] A "klick" equals 1000 meters.

[44] I've since learned that Army Rangers use a similar technique to this day.

Occasionally, Captain DeBona would open up a "beer tent" in the evenings for the non-combat and support troops, or for Marines who weren't currently on any sort of active status. I'd take advantage of those times when I could, but I wasn't a big drinker back then. Besides, the usual fare was a beer called "Black Label," and I never did get used to the taste. Too bad too, because, if I remember correctly, back then they were only like 5 cents a beer. Still, that was a lot for a PFC only making $120/ month (which included combat pay), and half of that I had taken out each month and sent back to Mom in an allotment check.

From time to time, someone would acquire a bottle of liquor and bring it back to the barracks, and we'd pass it around. What we'd normally get was a brand called "Silver Fox", which was supposed to be a premium vodka, but I think it was just a local rot gut, distilled in a barrel and poured into a bottle. It tasted horrible. I remember waking up one night and looking around the barracks. There, on the floor in the corner, was a nearly full bottle of Silver Fox. As I was staring at it, it exploded. Not a big or dramatic explosion; the bottle just seemed to break in half and spill on the floor. I remember going back to sleep and telling myself I would never have another sip of anything unless it was still in a sealed can from the states.

The "Brotherhood of the Bush"

This was also the time that I started to become aware that there was a small subculture in our platoon that was using their downtime to sneak off somewhere on the base and partake of the marijuana that always seemed to be available. I'd never used it before (or since), but I had to accept that it was just part of military life. What did I know? I was a kid from Iowa, still 18, and just starting to drink a little beer every now and then. I had no business even experimenting with stuff like that. Besides, most of the old regulars, like Sgt. Holley, would have kicked their asses across the squad bay if they ever showed up for duty with a confused look or slurred speech.

One afternoon I was sitting in the barracks, when in walked two of the newer replacements we'd gotten last month. I knew one of them, because he had been a member of my fire team for my short two-week command. I cannot remember his name.

Both men sat down in the bunk across from me and started making casual conversation. Eventually, I was invited to join them for one of the trips to their local hangout. I politely declined, but then they turned to the real reason they were there. Since I was in the barracks, or around the local area most of the time, and I had the platoon radio, they thought it would be "real decent" of me if I would give them a call if anyone was looking for them. One of their group (they called themselves the "Brotherhood of the Bush") was in charge of a squad radio, so he would be able to get the message right away.

They weren't very happy with my answer, "Look guys, these radio frequencies are monitored, so your plans aren't going to work. And besides, we're on 15-minute standby duty, and the first time Sgt. Holley sees either of you with those glassy-eyed stares, he's going to shoot your ass – or worse!"
This was a problem for me. I wanted to get along with everyone, and I especially had respect for anyone who had made it this far as a Marine, but, I was starting to realize, for the first time, that even though a lot of us go through the same challenges and hardships to get here, some were still the same assholes they were before they joined the Corp. After that I was a more careful who I made friends with, and I told these guys to get lost.

The Story of Sammy Vollmar

Sammy Vollmar was a young PFC, a replacement that came over from the States and joined Mike Company's 2nd platoon towards the last week of May while we were still at Phu Bai. I never knew Sammy personally. For that matter, I didn't really know anyone outside of my own 3rd platoon.

You may ask why I am writing now about Sammy Vollmar if I didn't actually know him. For two reasons: First, the incident I am about to describe happened in our company, right in the time frame when I was there, and second, because nearly 48 years later, Sammy's story reached out across time and touched several of our lives (myself, some of my buddies, and even our Company Commander, retired Lt. Colonel Anthony DeBona).

Let me start at the beginning. About a year ago, a young high school senior in Gillipsie County, Texas decided to write about Sammy for his senior project. The young student wanted to write about the day-to-day experiences of a combat soldier in Vietnam. Sammy's name was picked because he had been from the young student's own school, and because Sammy's name was memorialized in Gillipsie County as being the first from there to have died in the Vietnam War.

The student did some basic research about Sammy, found a website where historical records of our unit are kept[45], and got in touch with the webmaster, Nik Dunbar, who had served with Mike Company during the Siege of Khe Sanh. Nik contacted me, and between the two of us we were able to provide a lot of background information about Sammy's brief time with our unit.

Sammy's story goes like this: He graduated from high school in 1966, spent the summer having fun and trying to decide what he wanted to do with his life. He signed letters of intent to join the Marines Corps, but with a deferment so that he wouldn't have to begin training until the start of the next year.

On January 1st, 1967, Sammy was married to his high school sweetheart, and shortly thereafter, made his way to San Diego, California for basic training. Sammy graduated USMC boot camp,

---

[45] This is the website where a database is maintained containing the 3rd Battalion, 26th Regiment's Command Chronology records. It is an interactive database which can be searched by keywords or date, or both. http://www.326marinesinvietnam.com/

advanced to Basic Infantry Training School, and from there went to Advanced Infantry Training at Camp Pendleton.

A few days after graduating, Sammy was sent to Vietnam, and in the last week or so of May 1967, he joined our company as a Marine Rifleman, assigned to Mike Company, 2nd platoon.

Approximately a week later, on June 1st, 1967, Sammy was part of a 2nd platoon ambush, assigned to one of their LPs (listening posts). The LP was prematurely detected by a small group of VC. Automatic weapons fire was exchanged, and Sammy was killed. It was a very sad ending for such a promising and well-liked, young man.

Nik and I tried as hard as we could to give the young high school student information about what Sammy's daily activities were like. Fortunately, Nik's website provided direct access to our unit's day-to-day logs. Beyond that we supplied pictures of the barracks Sammy would have lived in, as well as some of the other activities he would have been involved with.

But, beyond the daily activities, I became interested in what had actually happened that night, even though the basic details were pretty clear cut. Nik's website logs provided map coordinates and times of the incident. Nik also has detailed tactical maps that helped me locate exactly where Sammy's platoon was when the ambush took place.

Sammy's platoon was set up on one side of a stream that came down a large hill and then forked in the flatland. The platoon was set up on the left fork of the stream. When Sammy's LP was detected and fired upon, the VC turned around and went back up into the hills before they could be followed.

At this point I became curious about where my platoon was when all of this happened. It turns out that we were located about 1 klick away, in a different location. The following night, however, we were set up in ambush along the very same stream, except that we were guarding the right fork, under the assumption that the VC group that had killed Sammy might try to come back down from the hills, but this time, use the right fork of the stream.

And that's exactly where we set up and were waiting when they walked through the next night. This time, however, the VC didn't detect our presence and walked right into the killing zone, and we zapped them. All of them!

As personally satisfying as this information was for us to know, Nik and I didn't feel it was appropriate for a high school writing project, so we just left that part out. We did, however share the story with some of the remaining veterans of our old group, including Andy DeBona, our old commanding officer.

Years ago, Andy had commissioned a bronze memorial plaque that displayed all the names of all the veterans who died while serving in 3/26 in Vietnam. Andy heard the story that Nik and I had pieced together, and that's when Andy noticed that Sammy's name had never been added to the memorial (possibly because he had only spent a few days in Vietnam). Andy wrote back to us, and personally assured us that Sammy's name was being added to the 3/26 Vietnam memorial plaque. This information we did share with the young student, as well as the assistant principal at his high school. We formally thanked them for their efforts, which finally saw that Sammy Vollmar's name was included on our Battalion's memorial site, and that he finally received the honor and recognition that he deserved. Semper Fi! (*Always Faithful!*)

The King's Tomb

We were still headquartered and working out of the Phu Bai combat base, and it would be another month before we made the move to Khe Sanh.

We received orders that the next morning the entire company would be moving out on a week-long operation, just to the north and west of Phu Bai and south of the city of Hue.

Hue was the old capital city of Vietnam. In the 1800-1900's, there had been a succession of kings who ruled Vietnam. They had built a series of their own royal tombs, much as the ancient Egyptian pharaohs built pyramids to be their shrines and tombs.

Most of these tombs were situated inside the official boundaries of the city, but a few were located miles south, beyond the banks of the Perfume River which borders the ancient city to the south. The tombs were quite elaborate, and consisted of courtyards, ornate terra cotta sculptures and statues, a palace area where the actual tomb resided, servant's quarters, and all surrounded by moats and bridges.

For the most part, during the war years, these tombs were abandoned but not desecrated or defiled by locals or enemy soldiers. The Vietnamese people were very superstitious about that, and tombs were treated as if they were holy ground. The Viet Cong would not even fire rifle or mortar shells at the tombs. Sometimes the Marines would take brief advantage of this fact by bivouacking overnight. However, not wanting to overdue a good thing, we would never spend an entire day there.

Mike Company had been out about 4 days already. We were working the area southwest of the old imperial city, running sweeps during the day, ambushes at night. The "hunting had been good." as our company commander liked to say, and the decision was made to stay out for a few more days.

In order to do that, we would need to be resupplied first. Resupplying an entire company in the field was no small matter. It would require several helicopters filled with C-rations, ammunition, and fresh water. Then there would be the inevitable "heat casualties" and anyone with minor wounds or injuries who would need to be sent back to the base. The whole process would take time to put together, so it was decided that we would push on to one of the tombs, named after "Khai Dinh." the king that was buried there. The tomb was built somewhat recently and completed in 1931.

[A long, broad stairway led to a courtyard, just in front of the palace. I slept that night in between the horse and the elephant that you see in this picture.]

In front of the main building was a giant courtyard with two opposing sets of life-sized, terra cotta statues that faced each other like opposing chess pieces. I slept between the statues of the elephant and the horse that night.

As we got within about a half mile of the tomb, we could begin to see its outline, located on a steep hill. My platoon was the second group to cross over the first of three small bridges that spanned concentric moats that surrounded the entire grounds.

There was dry, grassy ground all around the palace, and there were outbuildings which supposedly were used to house the servants and caretakers who managed the grounds. It looked as if it had been many years since anyone had occupied the buildings. As I mentioned, the entire area was treated deferentially by the locals. Still, it was evident from the inside of the mausoleum area that there had been some looting which had taken place.

All 3 platoons of Mike Company were spread out along the outside of the walls, on the grassy areas in front of the inner moat. The

[The tomb of Khai Ding. After crossing the last moat bridge, we were greeted by this magnificent stairway leading up to the mausoleum (or palace) area. The chessboard like figures are in the courtyard at the top of the stairs.]

command group, and the platoon leaders, along with their radiomen and all the FO's (forward observers), made their way up the giant staircase and took positions either in the courtyard or inside the main palace area itself.

The command group stayed inside the main palace area, so I selected a nice spot between one of the elephants and a horse in the main courtyard. I wasn't all that comfortable (security-wise) with the idea of sleeping out in the open like that, especially in such a high profile location, but when Lt. Manzi came out to inspect the gun positions and fire zones below, he assured me that we were quite safe there. He said it would be like being back home during the Civil War; no one would ever consider firing mortars at the burial site of George Washington.

Years later, out of curiosity, I did some research on Khai Dinh, and found out he was not a popular king at all. Instead, he was considered a mere puppet of the French government. To make matters worse, he increased national taxes nearly 30% just to help finance the construction of the palatial grounds where we were camped out.

The fact that no one fired upon us that night was probably due more to native superstition than anything else. Still, I felt secure and it was a peaceful night. I remember taking out a small flashlight and writing a long letter to Mom, describing in detail the architecture and grounds, and what it was like on the interior of the buildings. There had been some other events to write about as well.

Artillery Practice

Two days prior, there had been some real excitement. We had been walking along a river bank when we started taking heavy automatic weapons fire from the other side of the river. We immediately hunkered down and dug in.

This was not just a small group of VC, otherwise they would have broken it off after just a few minutes. We were receiving both small arms fire and the occasional RPG (rocket propelled grenades), but no heavy, 50-caliber or 60 mm mortar rounds, so this must have been a small company of VC with no heavy weapon teams.

Right away, Lt. Manzi called back to the command group and requested artillery. Command switched over to their FO (forward fire control officer) who brought 105 mm howitzer fire in from Phu Bai combat base, which was only few miles away. We had already taken a casualty in our first squad, so the lieutenant ran down to see how bad it was. He left me with the radio to help Fire Control with 'walking in' the incoming rounds. It was a pretty exciting time for me; this was the first time I gotten to do this.

The first round of artillery came in over the VC's heads and landed just behind them, but I wasn't exactly sure how far behind them. I'd been with the lieutenant before while he was adjusting mortar fire and had seen how he had done it. I'd also watched so many war movies as a kid that I felt pretty confident when I barked these orders back over the radio, "This is Mike-3, drop 50, drop 50"!

There was an uncomfortable silence, and I started to wonder if there was some protocol I was supposed to be using instead just trying to imitate Audi Murphy from the movie "To Hell and Back." A moment later I could hear another round was coming in. It landed much closer, but still, just a bit too far. Now I was starting to get into it. This was pretty cool, just like the movies. So I continued (doing an even better Audi Murphy impersonation), and I yelled over the handset, "That's it, Mack, now drop 50." and then 'Fire for Effect'"[46].

The next thing I noticed was that the artillery had stopped. "Oh crap." I thought. Now I was sure that I had screwed up and I started to think. "Oh damn, now I'm in trouble."
To make matters even worse, I didn't remember the call sign back to our FO. I imagined that he had to be standing close to the company commander, so I called for Captain DeBona's radioman. "Mike-1, Mike-1, this is Mike-3, over." Right away the Captain's radioman called back and said that they had lost contact with the artillery fire control in Phu Bai. I was told to "stand by."

It made sense. My radio, a PRC-25 only had an effective range of 1-2 miles. So, for that reason, I was relaying to our company forward observer, who was then relaying back to fire control at the base. For whatever reason, that connection had been lost.

We also had lost contact with the VC force across the river. They had broken off and run shortly after the first artillery shells landed. Since we were still on the opposite side of the river, and the closest viable crossing point for us was the direction we had been heading, we regrouped and continued on our way.

There had been a lot for me to write about that night, laying out comfortably on the courtyard of a king's tomb, on a cool, clear, and peaceful night in South Vietnam. Unfortunately, I never mailed that

[46] A term meaning that the adjustment/ranging is satisfactory, and to start firing at those ranging factors.

letter. Before we got back to Phu Bai, I had somehow lost it and the little Kodak instamatic camera that I had taken with me. The pictures you see here in the book were taken by someone else.

At the time I didn't know it, but in another few weeks we would be moving our base of operations to Khe Sanh, and then, several months after that to a forward fire base called Con Thien

I Think About Extending My Tour

I had recently been promoted to Lance Corporal (E-3), and I heard about a program where, if you signed up for a 6-month extension in Vietnam, you could get a 30-day leave to go back to the States I was considering that. I felt (naively) that I was now a veteran and had pretty much "seen it all." The next few months at Khe Sanh would disabuse me of any thoughts of "having seen it all."

The last 6 weeks had been particularly arduous for our company. One long succession of contacts with smaller groups of VC, and although we had been very successful, our losses were accumulating, mainly due to sniper fire and daily encounters with booby traps. There was even an instance where one of the Marines in our company nearly stepped into a bear trap. A BEAR TRAP! I didn't know they had bears over there, but evidently they did. In any case, some enterprising VC thought it might be a good idea to camouflage it, set it alongside the trail and see what he could catch.

When we finally got back to Phu Bai, the Captain knew our orders were going to be sending us to Khe Sanh soon, so he organized a little party for us. He said we could each have just 2 beers each, but it turned out there was enough to go around that most of us could have 3 or 4. Our 1st platoon hadn't gotten back yet from their rough rider duty and they missed out.

Rumors of Khe Sanh and the "Hill Fights"

I had been in Vietnam for several months now. We were starting to see some of the original members of 3/26, many who had become good friends, being transferred out to other units. The reason was pretty simple, our battalion had come over to Vietnam as a complete group, and therefor they would normally be rotating back (as a group) to the States, all at the same time. The problem this presented was that this would leave the remainder of the unit almost entirely devoid of any experienced men. In order to avoid this, some original members were being transferred out and replaced by newer replacements arriving from the States, or replacements who were coming from other Marine battalions.

From our platoon we were losing Bill Halsey and Gene Weresow, along with several others who had been strong leaders. They were now being transferred to 2/9 (2nd battalion, 9th marines). Fresh replacements, just beginning their 13-month VN tour, would be taking their place. George Eriksson, another original member of the platoon, had been severely wounded and was gone, recovering from multiple gunshot wounds. He had been sent to a hospital ship floating in the China Sea. Thankfully Eriksson would recover, he was a tough guy, but only after a lengthy and difficult rehabilitation process.

As replacements began filtering in, not all were greenhorns; some came from Marine units in the north that had been stationed at places like Khe Sanh, Lang Vei, and Con Thien. From them we began to hear stories and rumors that pointed to the fact that Marines in the forward fire bases were seeing a different kind of enemy, one that didn't run so easily, one that didn't mind going "toe-to-toe" with the Marines. Some rumors even made them out to be almost superhuman.

The NVA Soldier

These were the soldiers of the NVA (North Vietnamese Army). They were better armed and better trained. In contrast, the Viet Cong that we had been up against in the south were relying on more unconventional, guerrilla style warfare, hit-and-run. We had

[Mike Company beer party. The Company that had the most confirmed "kills" each month would drink for free. We obviously won this month.]

our share of experiences with them early on, in larger, company-size encounters, but lately those had come less often, and the VC losses had been very lop-sided in our favor.

It was a fact; we were now going to be meeting a more determined enemy. These meetings would be full-fledged encounters against a better organized, more determined enemy that brought with them heavier weapons, and something we hadn't seen as yet, artillery and rocket support from just across the DMZ (demilitarized zone).

[One thing that did surprise me when doing research for this book was that, although the NVA soldier did have all the advantages of better training, organization, and weapons, most of them had been drafted or conscripted from the cities and urban areas in the north. This meant that they were not as familiar with living and surviving in the jungles; as were their counterparts, the VC in the south.

In letters and captured documents subsequently studied after the war was over, it became apparent that for many, the long trip south along the Ho Chi Minh trail would be a nightmare and test of endurance that they had not foreseen. However, the letters that many of them wrote also showed that they had a very strong commitment to their cause, and they were willing to struggle and die for that cause. They were a very formidable enemy.]

The Move to Khe Sanh

The entire battalion was moving. This meant that H&S (command headquarters), 4 rifle companies (India, Kilo, Lima, and Mike), and our weapons company, Charlie Battery 1/13, which was part of our original Battalion Landing Team, would be packing up and moving.

The convoy consisted of 111 vehicles of all sorts, including jeeps, water tankers, ambulances, tanks, Ontos[47], personnel carriers, fuel trucks, and

The M-55 Quad 50 consisted of four Browning M2 .50-caliber machine guns, mounted in a power turret, on a 2-1/2 or 5 ton truck. With an effective rate of fire of 1000 to 1500 rounds per minute, nothing stood in its way. It was used primarily in perimeter defense and convoy protection, and it was more than adequate at providing defense against ground troop assaults.

[47] Lightly armored tracked vehicle with six 106 mm recoilless rifles. Had a three-man crew.

some wrecker trucks in case some of the vehicles got stuck along the way. We had four truck-mounted Quad 50's (pictured above) along for fire support and security. They were loaned to us courtesy of "D" Battery, 1st Battalion Air Defense. The Quad 50's were some real badass pieces of equipment. We even had a bridge team from 3rd engineers along in case we had issues during the long trek up Route 1, and then across Highway 9 to Khe Sanh.

Seeing an Old Friend

Our platoon was being loaded into a couple of open top, 6X6 trucks, and just as I was finding a place to sit up against the back of the cab, one of the Marines who had been riding shotgun came back to check to see that we were all secure. He was wearing sunglasses, but I would have recognized that face anywhere. It was Richard Light, who was a good friend of both myself and my younger brother Bob from back in our boot camp days.

"Hey, Pvt. Light." I yelled, "what the hell are you doing here? I thought you had a soft job back in the states." The last that I had heard, before I left for overseas duty, was that he had procured a cushy job driving a General around.

"Hey, Ward. Yep, I fell on some hard times and got stuck in Transport Company." Light replied. He didn't mention how or why he had fallen from grace, but knowing him, he would bounce right back. That was just his way. In boot camp he had been selected as our "*Right Guide*," a prestigious position in boot camp platoon. Then he lost that position, and then he got it back again. Same story, different day, but he was a very resilient guy.

He had a camera with him and took a shot of me in the truck, then had me take a picture of him. I had an un-mailed letter in my pocket that I was going to send to my brother Bob, and since it had both Bob's address (5th Tank Battalion, H&S Company) and my address, I just pulled the letter out and stuck it in my pocket and handed the envelope to Light with the instructions to send me back a copy of the pictures. That was all the time we had for talk, so we said our goodbyes, and then later, true to his word, I received a letter back from him about 6 weeks later with the pictures in it.

About midday, we passed by Dong Ha Base and Kilo Company and Charlie 1/13, our artillery battery, dropped off there to stay the night. Their orders were to continue on to Khe Sanh the following day. Our orders were to continue on to Khe Sanh and hopefully reach it by night fall, but along the way we received word that Highway 9 was impassable, due to a bridge being blown up by the VC. With no

[Note: I would see Light again two more times before I got out of the Marine Corps. He finally made his way back up to the rank of sergeant, which is amazing, because about the time we both came back from Vietnam, there was a freeze on promotions. I would bet that if he had stayed in the Marines Corps, he would have been a General before he retired.]

other choice, companies India, Lima, and Mike (my company) established night time positions in the hills, near the 3/3 (3rd Battalion, 3rd Regiment) command post. H&S Company spent the night at Camp Carrol.

The India, Lima, and Mike company perimeters were spread out a good 1000 meters apart but close enough to provide mutual support if needed. All I really remember about that night was that it was a very cold, rainy, and uncomfortable night. We dug temporary fighting holes and covered ourselves with our ponchos as best we could.

The next morning the engineers were still working on the bridge, so a decision was made by battalion headquarters to move Mike and Lima companies directly to Khe Sanh by helicopter. India and H&S

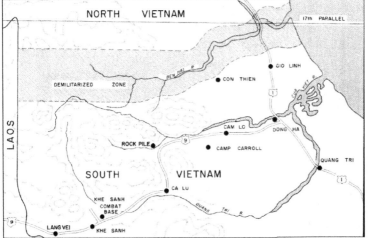

[The bridge that was blown was across Hwy9, just past the "Rock Pile." It would take several days for our engineers to repair.]

companies remained with the convoy until repairs to the bridge were completed. That was entirely fine with me, I was tired of riding in the trucks, and I was eager to get to our new home at Khe Sanh.

Chapter 8

Khe Sanh Combat Base

We were now on helicopters, and as ours cleared one of the final, tall hills, we could see the Khe Sanh base laid out before us. It was a spectacular sight to see. It was situated on a high, flat plateau, and surrounded by hills in all directions. There were sandbagged bunkers and concertina wire fences all around the entire perimeter. There was a runway for medium-sized planes, landing pads for helicopters, there were tanks and artillery emplacements. There were tents with high, sandbagged walls serving as mess halls and hospitals. Where Phu Bai had reminded me of a small city, Khe Sanh looked like a fortress built to withstand a siege[48].

Once both our companies[49] were completely off-loaded, instead of taking up new positions on the current base perimeter, we were marched to the west gate and continued on, past the perimeter for about 500 meters through old stands of tea trees and elephant grass that were 8-10 feet tall. I could see where a large military unit could easily hide there and not be seen until you were almost right upon them.

It took us almost an hour for both our companies to make our way through that mess. Once we cleared it, and came to a tree line, we began to dig in and set up a two-company, defensive perimeter where we would be spending that first night. Of course, it had to start raining again, and we were going to be forced to spend another miserable night out on that high, windswept plateau that was going to be our new home.

---

[48] Which, of course, it would soon be called upon to do. (In reference to the 78-day Siege of Khe Sanh in early 1968.)

[49] Kilo Company was still back at Dong Ha with the C 1/13 artillery battery and would catch up with the remaining convoy. India Company had stayed with the convoy until the bridge was repaired. Mike and Lima Company had already been flown to Khe Sanh by helicopter.

Our First Night at Khe Sanh

We had stopped to set up for the night. Lt. Manzi was meeting with
the Captain, so I proceeded to start digging a fighting hole
(sometimes called a "foxhole."). The soil was a fine, red dirt that
was easy to dig, but once I got down about a foot or so, it would start
caving in. To make things worse, when it was wet, it covered
everything it touched with a red-stained mud color. This was not
going to be easy or fun.

The hole I was digging was about 20 feet behind our new perimeter,
so I decided to erect a lean-to next to the hole using my poncho. I
trimmed branches from one of the small trees. The rain had stopped,
and my "little house" actually turned out to be pretty comfortable. I
still had my air mattress with my gear, so I blew that up and added it
as a nice finishing touch to my temporary living arrangements.

When the Lieutenant finally got back, he was dragging an extra
poncho liner with him that we laid down on the wet, muddy ground
underneath my lean-to. Surveying our handiwork, the Lieutenant
finally said, "Well, you're all set up for the night. I'll be at the
Command Post. Our Company Commander had a full blown
command tent that was set up well behind us in the tree line and this
meant that I had the whole lean-to to myself, and nothing to do but
monitor the radio. I didn't even have to stand a watch.

Since it was still somewhat light out, I fired up a heat tab[50] and
proceeded to cook one of my C-rations and make some coffee. After
my dinner, I pulled out a packet of Kool-Aid (Groovy Grape) and
made a cup full of "poor man's wine."

During the night I was awakened several times by artillery from the

---

[50] Since it was still light out, I could light a match to the heat tab, but no fires were allowed
when it was dark, so I took advantage of that fact and was able to have a hot meal, albeit, it
was still just a warmed up C-ration meal.

main camp. These "fire missions"[51] would sometimes last 15 or 20 minutes. It was difficult to hear myself think, let alone get some much needed sleep. It was just something we'd have to get used to. The next day I thought we'd finally be relocating to inside the perimeter at Khe Sanh, but instead we spent the whole day improving and building on our current positions. We stayed another night right where we'd been the first night. By now, India

 and Kilo Company had joined us at our position just outside of the Khe Sanh combat base. About 0500 the following morning, we heard an explosion, and then a short exchange of automatic gunfire on our left flank. It was coming from somewhere along India Company's portion of the perimeter line. A young Marine had heard a noise, got up out of his hole on the perimeter, and had been wounded by an incoming grenade. A short while later, India Company sent a squad out to sweep the area in front of that part of the line but found only footprints leading back into the elephant grass.

It would be another week before we'd finally be able to set up inside the actual perimeter at Khe Sanh. Our company, along with India Company, was preparing to sweep the nearby hills and valleys and get acquainted with this new, unfamiliar territory.

---

[51] A fire mission is when an artillery battery is firing at pre-arranged coordinates, with a specific number of rounds, or for a specific amount of time.

A Sea of Grass

The next morning, we did return briefly to inside the base perimeter, but only long enough so that both Mike and Kilo companies could march to the helipad area. From there we were transported to the top of a ridgeline along Hill 642. As our helicopter, a CH-46, which could carry about 17 combat troops at a time, waited in line to drop us off, we could see that the landing area was a heavy sea of elephant
grass. A line was starting to form at the back of our copter. I scooted in behind the Lieutenant, because I wanted to link up with him as soon as we got on the ground.

The Lieutenant was now at the end of the tail gate and it looked like he was just stepping off onto a green patch of grass. He took one step forward … and disappeared completely. Now it was my turn, and I was a little concerned. With a full pack and five day's provisions, and adding another 30 pounds for my radio and battery, I was like a huge, 250-pound bag of cement.

I hesitated just for a moment, and then stepped off the end. The drop was more than I expected. The grass must have been 8 or 9 feet high, and I landed with a tremendous thud. Somewhat stunned, I tried to get up, and then, out of nowhere, the Lieutenant's arm came out of the grass, grabbed my collar, and yanked me away just as the next Marine came crashing down. This was definitely something they hadn't trained us for.

Our platoon immediately formed up, and we started moving up the hill. Following the ridgeline across the top, we eventually came to a wide, grassy knoll. We spread out and set up a temporary perimeter while the rest of the company was still being off-loaded.

Aside from all the extra weight, you made a pretty distinctive target. But, even with that, I was starting to like being the Lieutenant's radioman. I was where the action was, and I got to know what was

happening right away. I was also remembering how, just a few months back, the radio had saved me from more serious injury when I landed in that punji trap. The terrain here was steep and tough going.

There were no trails to speak of, but there was a well-developed network of mountain streams and small rivers that ran through the valleys. Reading our tactical maps was much easier here in the highlands than it had been down in the Phu Bai area, which was dominated by large, open flatlands, filled with rice paddies.

In the South, judging your exact position within a topological map grid was more "guess-and-by-golly." but here in the highlands there were the ever present surrounding hilltops and intersecting waterways with which to orient yourself. Of course, we also had heavier vegetation and double and triple canopy ceilings that could make it extremely difficult. That's where the "step counting" training that the Lieutenant had given me would really came in handy.

Now that Mike and Kilo companies were off the helicopters, we split up to establish night defensive positions. Once that was done, each company would send out their own platoon-sized ambushes. Spreading our units out like this gave us a tremendous amount of flexibility to cover a very large area, and at the same time, one company could provide a blocking position if the other company flushed out groups of VC or NVA.

During the early morning hours, Mike Company's 2nd platoon's perimeter positions was probed. A single incoming grenade accounted for 3 Marines WIA (wounded in action), and two of them had to be medevacked out the next morning. After that, the wounded were picked up and our entire company began a general sweeping movement north. My 3rd platoon was descending downward, through an increasingly thick foliage of trees, towards the valley. The 1st platoon of Mike Company was already down on the valley floor from the night before where they had established a night ambush position. All 3 platoons of Mike Company were now operating independently, but still sweeping in the same direction.[52]

There were few trails to follow, so we had picked up on what seemed to be a popular animal trail that led through the thick jungle. There was a double canopy of tree limbs above us. The thick, still air and the irregular ground made the going even more slow and painful. It was exhausting. The foliage was so thick it was possible for two different groups of soldiers to be within 25 yards of each other and not even know it.

In the next few months we would start taking more casualties from

---

[52] It was a common practice for us, when our company was doing a sweep of a large area, to have all 3 platoons move towards different areas. In all instances, we would stay in contact with our company headquarters, as well as remain within a reasonable response distance should one or more platoons get into trouble.

heat exhaustion. More than we had from the booby traps we had run into when we were back in the lowlands around Phu Bai. Before we came to Khe Sanh, it was my habit to carry just two canteens of water, but we all soon got into the habit of taking 3 or 4.

Trial by Fire

It was about mid-morning of that same day when we heard a call over the radio that a wild fire had been started, and that it was rapidly burning through the elephant grass towards our position. The Lieutenant and I were in the middle of the column, and our platoon was at the tail end of the company, closest to the fire. I was told to check every 5 minutes with the rear squad (Rhett Holley's squad) to see how close it was getting. By now we were all bunched up, everyone trying to move as fast as they could. Sweltering heat and now the soot and ashes from the fire being blown in our direction made it hard to breathe.

Both Kilo and Mike Company were in its path, and it became a race against time to make our way to the valley floor and across one of the streams. It took another hour before both companies could be picked up and transported by helicopter to the top of Hill 642, where we reassembled. We established a defensive position near the top of the hill, and once again sent platoon-sized ambushes out for the night.

I've heard a couple of versions of what started the fire, but have found nothing in our Battalion Command Chronologies to support either. One version of the story is that our movements were spotted by enemy soldiers on one of the adjacent hills, and they had started the fire. Another, more likely version, is that the fire was started by a helicopter rocket assault which was taking place on an adjacent hill.

I was starting to realize that our new home here in the central highlands of Vietnam was going to present us with a new set of challenges, not the least of which was just getting from point A to point B. It seemed we were either climbing or descending steep, slippery hillsides, or we were fighting our way through dense underbrush. On the high plateaus and down on the valley floors, the razor-edged elephant grass could sometimes reach 15 feet high, making it nearly impossible to tell where you were, or even if you were right next to an enemy unit. I was probably the most nervous when we were walking through that tall stuff.

I had heard rumors that Lima Company had been walking through tall elephant grass and their point man ran right into the point man of an NVA company. A blazing gun battle erupted between both sides. The Marines started spreading out to their left and right to prevent any sort of flanking maneuver, and then advanced with shouts of "Fix Bayonets" filling the air. Evidently the enemy understood English well enough to realize they didn't want any part of that, and they turned around and went back the way that they had come.

Immediate pursuit would have been ill-advised, as it could possibly lead directly into an ambush. Helicopters were called in to raze the area with machine gun and rocket fire.

The final casualty count with Lima Company's contact with the enemy was 2 Marines WIA, 2 NVA killed, but it's impossible to tell what the final count really was. Every NVA platoon has one man carrying a long rope with meat hooks attached to drag away their dead. They were very aware that the U.S. military had a fixation on body counts, and they didn't want to give us that information.

In any case, our mission here at Khe Sanh had changed. Before, at Phu Bai, we were sweeping and ambushing at night. We were interdicting and disrupting the travel and flow of both communications and supply routes. Here at Khe Sanh, we were actively seeking out the enemy and picking fights. We would find areas where there had been recent activity, call in the information, and the coordinates would be marked for future bombing and artillery missions. All signs pointed to increased activity and increased troop sizes. The new strategy was to aggressively search them out and engage with them. Then we could call in air support, or the big guns from Khe Sanh and other nearby firebases like Dong Ha, C2, and Con Thien.

It was a dangerous game, and virtually guaranteed that there would be casualties when we went out, but the generals back at Division Headquarters had determined that the only way to engage the enemy was to go and seek them out. So far, the enemy had just been avoiding our combat bases.

The Stars Come Out at Khe Sanh

Two days later (June 27, 1967) we were finally back inside the actual perimeter at Khe Sanh. We had been a long time out in the bush, and though we had only engaged in light skirmishes with the enemy, we were finding evidence, almost on a daily basis, of NVA troop movement and activity. We would see fresh signs where platoon and company-sized elements of NVA had established night positions, in some cases leaving behind supplies and material that they could little afford to lose. This could mean only one thing, that they had left in a big hurry.

At times, our sweeps would take us right up to the Laotian border, or sometimes to the north, only a few miles away from the DMZ. We were on the very edge of the Ho Chi Minh trail, and it seemed like it was the height of NVA tourist season. Something indeed was brewing.

But for now, we were back at the Khe Sanh base and would have a few days (or longer) to rest up and get resupplied. We weren't exactly inside the old perimeter lines. We were given the task of clearing the brush and extending the perimeter out another 200 yards. Then we dug new fighting holes, building new bunkers, and setting up new, strategic fields of fire. Local Montagnard villagers were hired to help with clearing the elephant grass and vegetation. They probably did the work faster than we could have.

Manning the fighting holes was a twenty-four hour a day assignment, but we would do that in shifts, for only a few hours at a time. Squad leaders, platoon sergeants, and even the platoon commander would make regular checks of the line. Meanwhile, the rest of the platoon could take it easy, just behind the perimeter lines in the sandbagged bunkers we had built.

This left plenty of time to catch up on the dozens of little housekeeping chores that needed attending to after coming back from days in the field, such as; cleaning our rifles, darning our socks, writing letters home, and most of all, just catching up on sleep.

Khe Sanh Combat Base Map

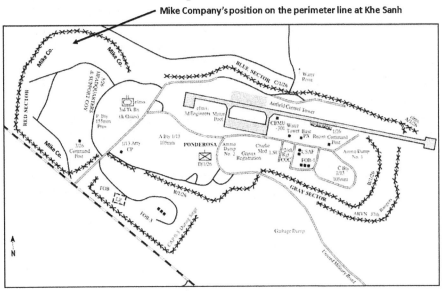

Mike Company's position on the perimeter line at Khe Sanh

There had been a command change several days prior, and our new regimental commander had visited the Khe Sanh base on the 25th, while we were still out in the field. I was sorry I missed that, because they said he visited the front perimeter lines to say hello to the troops. But he wasn't the only "celebrity" we would have a chance to see over the next few weeks.

Our section on the perimeter was next to the "Blue Sector," which guarded the air landing strip. The morning scuttlebutt was that we were going to get an impromptu visit from Hugh O'Brian (of "Wyatt Earp" television fame). He was also famous for having been the youngest drill instructor in the Marines Corps, at age 19.

Since I did not have perimeter guard duty that morning, I and a couple of buddies, hustled over to the Blue Sector and found a nice vantage point on top of a bunker. We just sat around waiting and watching. And there was no lack of entertainment that morning; the ARVN helicopter wing was letting some new pilot trainees practice their landings and takeoffs on the runway.

One pilot would make an approach and then try to come in for a soft landing, but he would hit the ground too hard, bouncing back up and forward, then down again and bounce again until he got to the end of the runway. The next pilot behind him would do the same thing. It almost looked like that was what they were trying to do until finally, someone got it right. The other helicopters were buzzing around like bees in a circle in obvious admiration of their new found "ace" pilot. They finally finished their drills, and all was quiet for a while.

About twenty minutes later we could see more activity taking place down at the airstrip. A jeep had pulled up, and there were several NCO's and one officer in a jeep. They were obviously waiting for someone. We didn't have to wait long to find out who it was. Two Hueys[53] landed together, and out came several men; one was Hugh O'Brian. They were all wearing green jungle fatigues, and he was impossible to miss. He looked just like Wyatt Earp. Hugh O'Brian and the officer in the jeep shook hands, and then there was a short conversation. Suddenly, Mr. O'Brian and his group turned and jogged back to the helicopter, and they just flew off. What a disappointment! I had the distinct impression that Hugh O'Brian was just as disappointed as we were, but I guess plans had changed. That's the Marine Corps; plans are always changing. ("Same shit, different day!")

But that didn't turn out to be the only brush with celebrity I would have while I was there. It was several weeks later. Our company was once again on perimeter duty; our shifts were being changed every

---

[53] A military helicopter powered by a single turboshaft engine, with two-bladed main and tail rotors.

four hours, and I had drawn an early evening shift. Now they were putting two of us in each fighting hole, but we were short of men, so I was in a fighting hole by myself. The other half of our platoon was in the sandbagged bunkers about 20 yards behind us.

It was dark that night, and quiet. No flares had popped off, and being somewhat bored, I happened to look behind me. I saw three Marines jogging down to the line where we were at. They stopped at the hole just to my left and one of the guys squatted down and was talking to the two Marines in that fighting hole. I wondered what it was all about, but couldn't catch what they were saying. After a short, animated conversation, he shook their hands and then came over to my hole, followed by his two escorts.

I could see the guy who was doing all the talking. He wasn't armed, like the other two men, but he was wearing green jungle fatigues and no insignia. Before I had chance to say anything, he turned and asked if he could climb down in the hole with me.

"Sure," I said, and he jumped right in. He took off his helmet, and I immediately recognized him; it was William Holden.

Flabbergasted, I just sat there with this big, moronic smile on my face. I tried to say something, but nothing was coming out of my mouth. My brain was still dealing with the total improbability of it all.

Finally I said, "Hi, Mr. Holden!" He replied back with a big smile on his face and he said, "I just wanted to tell you that we're all very proud of you and the job you're doing over here." I think he was waiting for a reply, but my mind was racing furiously, trying to think of something appropriate to say.

I just sat there with that dumb smile on my face. For the life of me, I couldn't remember any of the movies he had been in. And then, I suddenly thought about "The Bridge Over the River Kwai," but my brain wasn't fully convinced that he'd been in that one.[54]

I finally came up with this, "Can I offer you anything, Mr. Holden?" That was a really dumb thing to say, not the least bit because I had nothing to offer him. I was in that dark, muddy hole, and except for a canteen full of dirty river water that I hadn't dumped out yet from our last field mission, I really had nothing to offer him. I couldn't even remember if I'd put halizone tablets in my canteen.

So, while I'm still fumbling around for something to say, Mr. Holden finally said, "Is there anything you need, anything I can get for you?" I knew how to answer that, "No sir, I have everything I need, but thank you very much."

And with that he just smiled back, shook my hand, and said, "Good Luck!" Next thing I know he's on his way to the next hole, but before he got there, the two men who were accompanying him said something, and they all walked briskly back up the hill to Command Headquarters.

As I sat there in the dark, contemplating what had just taken place, and mentally kicking myself in the butt for being so star-struck that I couldn't even make a decent conversation, I started thinking about the last thing he had said to me, "Good luck!" and I was wondering if he had meant that for me, or if it was instead a silent prayer said for the whole war effort if they had guys like me on the front lines. I'll never know for sure, but I do know this, he sure was a nice guy.

Whatever the reasons that brought him there, I had to appreciate the fact that he had come all that way, with no public fanfare, to sit in a fighting hole, on the outer most front lines at Khe Sanh, which was arguably one of the most dangerous places on the face of the earth, just to say to me, "Thank you for your service."

Semper Fi, Bill Holden

---

[54] It had actually been one of William Holden's best movies.

My .45 Pistol Has a Curse

It was about this time that I decided that I needed to acquire a pistol to carry along in addition to my M-16. It seemed only natural. I had seen other radiomen carrying them, but because I was still considered a "grunt" (a rifleman), I was never issued one. I didn't want to ask the Lieutenant for one, because I was sure he would have felt it was unnecessary. So, I did the next best thing, I asked Rick Szabo, our unofficial platoon scrounger, to see if he could acquire me one.

I was both pleased and surprised when, the very next day, Rick had one ready for me to look at. Rick said I could have it, along with a holster and an ammunition clip, for just $50. I wasn't expecting for him to come up with it that quickly, so I apologized and said I wouldn't be able to pay for it until next payday. I should have known something wasn't right when he blithely said, "No problem, I trust you." The reason I should have been a little suspicious was that Rick was a hustler, and, as it turned out, the gun in question happened to have a "curse" on it.

A little background on the "curse claim" is in order. The gun did have some history behind it. Rick had acquired it early on when the battalion first landed in Vietnam on December 11, 1967. At some point there was an accident, and Rick had ended up accidently shooting himself in the leg with that same .45. He had to be sent down to a hospital in Da Nang for about a month until he recovered well enough to rejoin the platoon.

Then, six months later, there was another incident involving that same gun. In the picture below are, Sgt. Lund, Cpl. Fossell, and Rick Szabo. Sgt. Lund said to Rick, "Hey Rick, let me see that pistol you shot yourself with." A few minutes after this picture was taken, Sgt. Lund managed to accidently shot himself in the leg, and I think that was the last time we saw him. He never came back to the platoon.

It was shortly after Sgt. Lund's mishap that I asked Szabo if he knew where I could get a .45. Given its history, I assume he was only too happy to get rid of it. Unfortunately, I only learned about the 45's history later.

[Sgt. Lund (on the left), with Fossell and Szabo. (Picture courtesy of Sgt.Rhett Holley.)]

About a week after getting my new .45, we were out in the field again. We were part of a company effort to clear the top of one of the many hills in the area that we only knew by a number designation. Our job was to secure the top of the hill, while the 1st and 2nd platoons were to provide blocking positions on the other side. We were slowly moving up the east slope.

We knew from recent Recon reports that the VC had had a defensive position on the hilltop, and had been firing mortars towards the Khe Sanh base. It was thought that they had moved by now, but there was always the possibility of stragglers or snipers who had stayed behind. Given those conditions, there was only one safe way to approach the hilltop, and that was with a full assault up the face, spread out in a skirmish line, with guns blazing. As it turned out, there were still 3 VC at the top who briefly opened up with harassing fire, but they soon left down the opposite side of the hill, where they ran into the rest of our company.

As my platoon was still advancing upwards, it was quite a dramatic scene. The skirmish line of Marines advancing, firing M-16s from the hip. I kind of got caught up in it all, and at one point I lowered my M-16, reached under my flak jacket, whipped out my .45, and started blasting away at the hill top. I think I probably looked like "Hoot Gibson" in a bad cowboy movie. I'd fired 3 or 4 shots in this manner when I turned to see what the Lieutenant was doing. He was standing there, one hand on his hip, and just staring at me.

"Ward, what the hell are you doing?" And with that, he just shook his head and said, "We'll talk about this later," and he went back to directing our platoon up the hill. I was kind of relieved in a way. I knew he'd eventually spot the .45, even though I was hiding it under my flak jacket. The Lieutenant was pretty strict about not carrying unauthorized weapons.

One time, one of the guys had latched on to an AK-47, and was keeping it stored in his duffel bag when we were back in Phu Bai. The Lieutenant found out and got pretty upset and made him turn it in.

I expected that the worst that would happen was that I was going to have to turn in my .45. Instead, I was surprised when the Lieutenant told me that if I wanted to keep it, I'd have to learn how to disassemble and clean it correctly, and he gave me a short class on how to do that.

So far, so good, you would think, but that wasn't to be. The pistol still had a curse on it, and it wasn't done yet.

It was one evening, not that long after my "Hoot Gibson" on the hill episode. We were in the field, set up in our standard ambush position. The Lieutenant, myself, and our corpsman, "Doc"

O'Connell,[55] had all taken up a position behind a large rock. Doc, I, and the Lieutenant would usually take turns monitoring the radio at night, but right then, none of us were sleeping, so I thought it would be a good time to get out my .45 and give it a quick cleaning. Doc saw me doing this, so he pulled out his .45 and decided to clean his as well.

Doc pulled back the slide on his .45 to make sure there was no round in the chamber. Unfortunately, the clip was still in his gun, so when he let the slide go, it fed a round into the chamber and the gun accidently went off. The .45 round just missed my head, but did strike a glancing blow and put a dent in my helmet. I was sitting on my pack at the time, and it knocked me completely over. Both Doc and the Lieutenant thought I'd been killed. I was lying on the ground, pretty sure that I'd been hit right between the eyes, and I was just waiting for my life to start flashing by.

When I realized that I was still alive, I started feeling around to see if I still had ears and a nose and if there was any blood on my face. Nothing, except a terrible ringing in my ears, which wasn't helped by all the yelling that the Lieutenant was now directing at Doc. It wasn't really Doc's fault though. Now I knew for sure that my .45 had a curse on it, and somehow, it had infected Doc's gun as well. After that we were both were extra careful when we cleaned our weapons, and I was never completely comfortable carrying the .45 after that. But, I wasn't about to get rid of it either.

The Montagnards

The Montagnards, also known as the Degar, are the indigenous peoples of the Central Highlands in South Vietnam. The name itself means "mountain people." My unit had not encountered them prior

---

[55] The corpsmen were actually Navy medics attached to Marine units to provide emergency medical care in the field to wounded Marines. This meant they came under the same fire as the Marines they were assigned to, and at the call of "corpsman!" they ran to the aid of the wounded soldiers. Many deservedly received commendations for bravery. They were inevitably referred to as "Doc".

to moving to Khe Sanh. The Army Special Forces had begun using them several years earlier because of their familiarity with the area and also for their well-known skills as both scouts and trackers. When the Marines Corps began establishing forward fire bases in the Central Highlands, it became common for us to employ them as well. Eventually, a deep respect developed between the Montagnards and the Marines.

The Montagnards were considered to be a "minority people." and were often shunned or ostracized by the main population of Vietnamese. We found them to be tremendously loyal, absolutely fearless, and generally friendly when we would work with them. It was in early July that I first saw a Montagnard village. Their dwellings were elevated above ground to keep out snakes and other pests, as well as to provide a form of air conditioning through the hot months of the dry season, and faster drying out during the rainy season.

[*Standing by as our Lt. Manzi negotiates to recruit 2 scouts from the village. This is a "Bru" tribal village, one of the 30-odd different tribes that make up the Montagnard populations in the Central Highlands.*]

Many of the young Montagnard men were already working directly with Army Special Forces teams, who would provide them with training, weapons, and uniforms. They were sometimes referred to as "tiger scouts," because of the distinctive camouflage patterns on their jungle uniforms

[I was very impressed; some of the huts were quite elaborate.]

We were looking to temporarily hire 2 scouts to help lead us through this new, unfamiliar territory. We had been told that we could trust the Montagnards, and although many of the able-bodied men in the village were away, there were always villagers who were willing to take on a few day's work.

We hired 2 scouts to work with us. They walked point and were very impressive to watch. The younger one (maybe 14 or 15 years old) was carrying a small crossbow, and the other, older villager, had a .30 caliber carbine. When we stopped to take a break. I broke out some C-rations and offered a package of crackers and cheese to the younger Montagnard, but he just shook his head. Sgt. Holley was looking on, and he said to me, "Don't mess with the Montagnards, Ward. If he gets hungry, he'll just kill something with that crossbow of his."

Many of the Montagnards who had been trained by the Army Special Forces carried M-16's which had been supplied by the Army, or AK-47's that they had taken off dead NVA. Although our scouts were just ordinary villagers, they were more than adequate to the task. The Montagnards claimed that they could actually tell the difference in smell between the North and South Vietnamese Armies, even though, they said that they both "smelled bad"[56].

Montargnard soldiers at a Special Force Camp. After Vietnamization program, most of the camps were put under ARVN's reponsibility, and the ethnic soldiers were considered as Rangers.

[*From "Remembering the ARVN." http://www.vnafmamn.com/ARVN_soldier.html]*

The French War Correspondent

It was somewhere about this time (July or early August) that we picked up a French magazine correspondent who went out into the field with us. The correspondent was a woman, in her 30s I'd guess, with dark hair and she had a seasoned look about her, partially because she was missing her left arm. I could only imagine how that might have happened. She was also quite attractive (Or maybe, I'd just been in the field too long.).

---

[56] Although the Montagnards were treated poorly by their Vietnamese brothers, at the same time, they were generally left alone by local VC because of their fierce and independent nature.

She first joined our platoon when a helicopter came in with resupplies for our company command post. My platoon was sweeping the valley area that day around Hill 758, and she was embedded in our platoon. When we started out, she stayed in the middle of the column, right behind the Lieutenant, and I was walking right behind her. I noticed that she was carrying a different kind of pack. It was an NVA rucksack, much prized by American forces, because they were so light, yet versatile (It had 3 small, outer pouches, and a durable cloth main pack, which made it lighter to carry than our own). She never talked or said a word except for the times we might be taking a break, and then she and the Lieutenant would huddle together, usually looking at his tactical maps. It was obvious that this wasn't her first patrol.

We didn't set up an ambush that night, but instead returned to the company's defensive perimeter, and I never saw her after that. I wish I had caught her name, it would be interesting, years later, to read about some of the work she had done.

So now, just in the last 5 or 6 weeks, we'd had a visit from the battalion commander, had two movie stars drop in, and a visit from a mysterious and beautiful war correspondent. Throw in the fact that we were now having more frequent encounters with larger and larger groups of well-trained and determined fighters, and you would have to say to yourself, "Well, at least I'm living in interesting times." I was beginning to think that things could not possibly get any stranger than this, I mean, what else could we expect, a circus coming to town?

The Circus Comes to Town

So far I haven't spoken much about some of the more exotic mammals and reptiles that we encountered (and there were more than a few), but there were a couple of incidents that involved me directly, and I need to mention them here. They all happened while we were working out in the field near the Khe Sanh base. They both happened on the same day; sometime in August of 1967.

Early on in my tour, about the same time we received our new M-16's, we got a lecture on poisonous snakes in Vietnam. There had been many rumors floating around about encounters with the deadly "3-step snake." This was a snake supposedly so deadly that, once bitten, you would be dead before you could take just 3 steps. This, it turns out, was just a myth. Even the deadly king cobra, which can reach lengths of up to 15 feet, does not kill you that quickly. But, if your mind believes something strongly enough, it just could happen, and this was becoming a big enough problem for the Marines Corps that they decided some education into the subject was called for.

As with all good ideas that come from higher up the command chain, this idea came with unintended consequences. While listening to the lectures, we were relieved to hear that the "3-step snake" was not real. But we also learned that the most poisonous of the snakes could still kill you in a short period of time, just not in 3 steps. The question was raised, "Do our corpsman carry the antidotes out in the field?" The answer was, "Well, no, that would be impossible." The next question was, "Well, would a medevac helicopter be able to get us back to an aid station in time?" The answer was, "Probably, yes … well, maybe sometimes… but most of the aide stations don't have all the antidotes either."

One bright young Marine popped up, "Well, if that's the case, then I wish there really was a "3-step snake." Sounds like it would save us all a lot of pain and agony."

The Asian Cobra

These incidents took place just a few weeks before I went on *R&R* [57]. The 3 platoons of Mike Company were flown by helicopter from Khe Sanh to a destination just a few miles south of the combat base.

---

[57] R&R stands for "Rest & Recuperation" and was a one-week period of leave allotted to any serviceman who had been in Vietnam for 6 months or more. There were a limited number of destinations that were approved.

It was to be a week-long campaign, and the object was to find and engage the enemy; nothing more, nothing less. When we first landed, we set about digging fighting holes and establishing a defensive perimeter. Our command and weapons teams were placed in the center. Once the perimeter was established, M60 machine gun squads were positioned just behind the perimeter fighting holes, on the rising slope about 20 feet back.

[Cpl. Randy "Ziggy" Zigienfuss, setting up his M-60 machine gun.]

It was still early afternoon, and my platoon wouldn't be moving out until just before dark. We had been ordered to establish a night time ambush site about 1000 meters from our current, temporary position. The lieutenant and I had found a nice grassy spot to set up. It was between, and slightly forward, of two of the machine gun positions. The lieutenant left me with the radio and his pack and gear, while he went back up the hill to the command post to confer with Captain DeBona about tonight's mission.

I found myself with a few hours to just relax, kick back in the soft, three-foot high grass, and just take it easy. It was a beautiful, sunny afternoon with a light breeze and clear sky, perfect for just lying flat on your back, watching the clouds float by, and daydreaming about my upcoming R&R in Taipei, Taiwan.

I'd been lying there, flat on my back, in the deep grass for maybe about 20 minutes when I heard something moving through the grass, and then I felt something bump into my right hip. Startled, I rose up and turned my head to my right to see what it was. As I turned my head, I could see something, just a shadow, rising out of the grass at the same time. The thing in the grass was just as startled as I was. Staring directly into my eyes, just inches away from my face, was a large Asian cobra. Hood flared out, mouth just beginning to open, and what I can only assume was a look of general surprise on its face.

Years later, I would read more about cobras, and I would estimate that this guy must have been between 6-8 feet long. A cobra can only raise up about 1/3 of its body length. Since the snake's head had been exactly eye level with me, I was able to estimate his size from that. The scariest thing I read about them was that the Asian cobra is also capable of spitting its venom; they are very accurate, and the primary target will be your eyes.

At the very moment I sat up, my mind still hadn't fully grasped what I was looking at. Just as the snake had started to open its mouth, I was already moving. I still cannot recall getting up. It must have been the primitive part of my brain was giving the orders directly

to my leg muscles. Even before the fear was fully registering in my mind, I was running in the opposite direction as fast as I could, and imagining the snake was right behind me. I expected at any second to feel a strike to the back of my leg.

I probably would not have stopped running except for the sudden, staccato sound of machine gun fire behind me. I heard other Marines, all starting to shout at once, and then the firing ceased.

I stopped and looked around. I first wanted to make sure the snake wasn't still chasing me. Then, when I realized it wasn't, I looked up and saw one of our machine gunners, with his M60 cradled firmly in his arms, pointing and shouting excitedly at a spot in the grass, in the opposite direction from where I had been running.

By now, a small crowd was gathering around the gunner, everyone asking him what had just happened. He pointed at me and said, "I was just sitting at my gun when I saw this guy (*and he pointed at me*) rise up, and this huge, really freakin' huge, snake lifted up up out of the grass right beside him. Next thing I know, this guy takes off in one direction, and the snake in another. That's when I picked up my gun and I went after the snake." The gunner took a deep breath, and then he continued, "I could see the grass moving where the damn snake was trying to get away and I just started firing."

You can image how this must have scared all the Marines who were right in front of him. They were just sitting there in their fighting holes, eyes forward, and suddenly a machine gun opens up *right behind them*.

Just then, the Lieutenant was coming back from his briefing, and after listening to everyone's version of the events, he finally restored order. The Lieutenant started to walk back towards the command post to report what all the firing was about, when he turned and yelled at me, "Jesus, Ward, I can't leave you alone for a minute!" I was still so shaken by the whole thing that I didn't even pay attention to him. But, I didn't lie back down in the grass after that either.

The Scout Dog and the Tiger

Later that afternoon, with the approach of darkness, we began to form up the platoon to go out on our night mission. We hiked down the hillside towards the dense jungle near the valley floor. Our plan was a simple one; we would quietly make our way to a location about 1000 meters from base camp, set up just off the trail about 20 yards, and set a nighttime ambush.

This night would be our first time working with a military scout dog. The dog and his handler were both specially trained, and they worked together to alert us if they detected the presence any enemy troops. Surprisingly, the dog was also trained to detect trip wires and explosives. This was a huge plus for us, since we would be moving along an unfamiliar jungle trail, and we would be moving in near total darkness.

Most of us had seen dogs used on base security before, but what was different about these scout dogs was that they had been trained never to bark or make much noise. Instead, they would communicate to the handler that something was wrong, and even to some extent, who and what they were detecting.

The Lieutenant and I were positioned in the middle part of the column with our 2nd squad. Things seemed to be going well. We had slipped outside the perimeter and crossed the open stretch of land with no problems. We then picked up the trail right where the tree line began. After having traveled about half of the distance to our intended ambush position, something happened that made us all freeze in our tracks.

The dog had started barking, and it wasn't normal barking either, it was a long, loud series of low, frenzied growls, barks, and high-pitched squeals. We could hear the handler shouting at the dog, trying to calm him, and then, we heard a nerve shattering roar that just seemed to fill the whole night.

Just then, our point man (just behind the dog and handler) started firing his M-16. And then another M-16 joined in. The dog was now barking in an almost hysterical manner.

Lieutenant Manzi rushed to move up to the front of the column. A normal reaction of the Marines in front of him would have been to get into a low crouch and start moving forward as well, towards the sound, but instead, they were huddling up in little groups. The lieutenant was pushing past them shouting, "Spread out! Spread out!" I was following as best I could, directly behind him, bumping and shoving into startled Marines.

When I finally made it to the front of the column, the Lieutenant and the squad leader were crouched down, rifles pointing into the dense brush just off to their right. It was pretty evident to everyone by now that the dog had flushed out a tiger. Just as that was starting to sink into my head, a call came over the radio.

"Mike-3, Mike-3, what's your status?" I answered, "Hang on, I'm putting the Lieutenant on." and with that, I passed the handset over to him. The Lieutenant explained briefly what was happening, and after a few minutes of discussion with our Company Commander, he had me call to the radioman at the rear of our column, and tell him that we needed to turn around. We were heading back to the base perimeter. The mission had been compromised by all the noise, racket, and gunfire, and there would be no ambush that night. And, we had no intentions of going back into the bush, looking for a wounded tiger.

The Lieutenant ordered the dog handler to stay in the back of the column, figuring that if the big cat did come back, those two be the first to know it. The Lieutenant's last words to his rear squad leader were, *"If the tiger comes back, shoot him. And if that damn dog starts barking again, shoot him too!"*

I'm sure the Lieutenant didn't mean it. I'm sure he was just frustrated that we had to scrub the mission. In any case, we weren't about to shoot the dog.

Surrounded by the NVA

It was the day after the aborted night ambush. The Lieutenant called a meeting of his three squad leaders to go over the plans for the next two nights. Mike Company was going to split up all three of its platoons, and each would independently set out to establish its own individual ambush positions for the night. This is how we normally operated, so no surprise there.

The DMZ[58] was just two miles north of us, and we were perilously close to the Laotian border. Recon platoons had discovered what looked like a heavily traveled pathway, and they suspected it was being used by the NVA to move troops and heavy equipment to strategic points around the Khe Sanh base.

As the lieutenant explained his plan to his squad leaders, it became evident that Battalion Headquarters was pushing for a much more aggressive approach for locating and engaging the enemy. Normally, each platoon would establish their ambush locations, then send out a 2-man LP[59] on each flank for an early warning. The LPs would have orders not to fire when they saw the enemy, but only to radio in that "bad guys" were coming. After that, the LPs would act as a blocking element if any of the enemy would try to escape.

Although that would be what we would "normally" do, it would be very different this time. The orders were that the LPs would now be 4-man groups (instead of 2), and they would go out a considerable distance further than ever before, approximately 1000 or more meters. Since the LP would now be a full fire team (consisting of 4 men), the LP would be given the flexibility to initiate an ambush *if they felt they could handle the enemy force*. No need to call in for permission, just do it.

The tacticians back at Battalion Headquarters evidently felt this would be a new and effective way to spread an ever larger net, and thereby to increase their body counts, which was how they measured

---

[58] Demilitarized Zone that divided North Vietnam from South Vietnam.

[59] Listening Posts

their degrees of success or failure. After this night, it would become apparent to everyone that this was not one of their brighter plans.

Our entire 3rd platoon set out around mid-morning to our designated position. When we arrived, we set up alongside the trail. The Lieutenant once again called his squad leaders and had them assemble the two new, 4-man, forward and rear LP teams. I was assigned to carry the radio for one of the teams. Lieutenant Manzi stayed with our 3rd squad (His radio call sign now would be "Mike 3-3." because he was embedded within our 3rd squad.). The radio I was carrying would now be designated as "LP-2."

I always thought I was chosen for this mission, because I was now the most experienced radio operator in the platoon, but in hindsight, I believe it was simply because I was the "step counter." I believe that it was critical that the Lieutenant know exactly where we were because we were very, very close to the Laotian border. As it turned out, our LP would go out approximately 1000 meters west, and just inside of the Laotian border. It would also be very close to the Ho Chi Minh Trail, but none of that was ever really discussed with us.

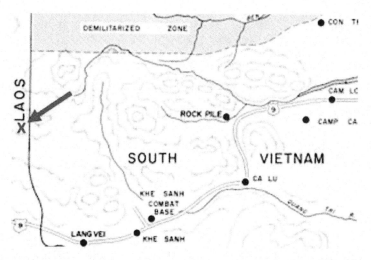

[Murphy and I and the other two members of the Listening Post ended up being just inside the Laotian border, and the rest of our unit was 1000 meters on the other side of the border, in Vietnam territory. I don't believe that was intentional, but that is how we ended being right on the edge of the NVA's main supply route coming down the Ho Chi Minh Trail.]

- *These notes are from the 3/26 Command Chronologies and they give a very brief overview of the events that followed. The date stamp 08111935 refers to Aug 11, 1967 at approximately 7:35 P.M.*

- *The notation in the Command Chronology refers to "3 platoon-sized infantry elements", which meant it was an intact NVA company, probably escorting an additional weapons platoon, and with light artillery which was to be positioned somewhere around the Khe Sanh combat base.*

1935H: A Mike 3 LP at XD782396 observed an estimated platoon-sized element of NVA approach their position from the west. The element moved passed the LP towards Mike Companys position at XD794398. Two other platoon sized elements following the first set op for the night in a semi-circle within 10 meters of the LP position.
0200H: The Mike 3 LP checked off the company net until 0200H when it reported the above the above information to Mike Company. India Company and Huey gunships were placed on standby.
0500H: The LP was still encircled being well concealed on a ridge above the draw in which the NVA were located.
0515H: Mike Company moved to positions to take the enemy under fire should they move: Mike 2 moved to XD788403 and Mike 3 prepared to follow the enemy to the east and block their wit drawl if they made contact with Mike 1 or Mike 2.
0950H: The LP reported no movement or sounds from the NVA for the last 15 minutes.
1030H: Mike 3 arrived at the LP position at 1030H and found that the NVA had moved at 1010H dragging something heavy at ????H an AO arrived on station and artillery was fired was fired at the vicinity of XD775395 to ???? the enemy withdrawal. Mike 3 trailed the NVA but never sighted the enemy.

[Those were the official notes in our Command Chronology, but the actual facts were a lot more dramatic than that.]

When my LP team began to first move out to get to our new position, I was instructed to call back every 15 minutes with my step count. When we finally reached a good spot, we called back to the platoon, and were told to set up for the night and make status reports every 30 minutes.

We thought we had found a good location. It was 20 meters off the trail and had a great view of a flat, grassy area that opened up from the heavily wooded area just to the west, where another trail made a "T" of sorts. The trail continued on south, but also broke off to travel the direction that we had just come from (towards Khe Sanh). It seems that we were at a junction. If someone was going to head for Khe Sanh, they would go the direction we had just come from. If they were going south, they would take the fork, and Mike Company already had another platoon in that direction to act as a blocking force. If they turned and went back the way they came, they would be heading back across the Laotian border.

There were a few, minor problems with the spot we had chosen. It was a large, thick, bush with an embankment behind it, but we were positioned far enough off the trail so as not to be easily seen. It gave a clear view of everything, but if for some reason we had to withdraw, we would have to do it to one side of the bush or the other. Due to the hill at our back, that was not a viable escape route. On the plus side, we were able to space ourselves a few yards apart, and to dig shallow fighting holes from which to fire if need be.

It was now around 6:30 PM and just starting to get dark. I called in and made a radio check to "Mike 3-3." Sgt. Holley, who was the leader of 3rd squad, and was monitoring the radio. Lt. Manzi was with him.

Our 4-man team consisted of our team leader, Cpl. Murray, myself, and two other Marines from Sgt. Holley's squad. All was quiet for the first thirty minutes. Then, just as I was getting ready to make the next check-in call, Murray spotted someone coming down the trail from the west (from the Laotian border side). We were all watching intensely. After the first man, a second enemy soldier came into view, and then a third, and more were still coming. We got down as flat on the ground as we could and started counting legs, because that's all we could see.

We had already talked about how we would handle this situation if it came up. If there were four or fewer people, the Marine on the left (that was me) would take out the lead man. Murray, who was next to me, would take the next man and so on until our man on the right end of the LP would take the last man on the trail. If there were 5 or 6 or 7 or more men, then we'd work both ends in towards the middle, that way the last man at the end of their column wouldn't get away. If there were more than that, we would let them go and call it in for one of our blocking elements to handle them. No sense biting off more than we could chew. We'd handled much larger groups than this, but never with just a 4-man fire team.

The enemy body count was now over a dozen, and we were all starting to get really nervous. This was a large group, and they were NVA. We just needed to be very quiet and still until they'd all passed. Then we would call it in, and hopefully, after that, we'd be joining up with our platoon.

But the NVA soldiers just kept coming until we finally had counted nearly 30. I was taking short, shallow breaths now, and I could hear my heart pounding in my ears. I was just waiting for their column to clear the open space and start moving away from us, so I could call back to report this to the Lieutenant.

We finally were able to make the call, and reported that "a platoon-sized group of NVA had just walked past us, heading south." But then, just at that moment, another group started coming into the clearing from the west, walking in the same direction as the first group. It was evident that they were all part of a much larger group.

Now we were all getting scared. Just how many of them were there? We were hugging the ground and no longer counting bodies. We were just looking at a mass of feet moving along the trail. Murray gently grabbed the handset of the radio and whispered, "Mike 3-3, Mike 3-3." we now have more NVA, possibly another platoon, and they've stopped on the trail, right in front of us"

There was no immediate response from the radio. Murray tucked the handset inside his shirt to muffle the sound of his voice. I realized we were also going to have another very serious problem with the radio "squelch." The squelch is a sound that a 2-way radio makes when the carrier signal goes below a certain threshold. There was no way to try to adjust it without potentially causing it to "sound off" while we were fumbling with the squelch control. Turn the knob left, or turn the knob right? It was like a scene from a movie where the good guy had to decide whether to cut the green wire or the blue one. Choose wrong and everybody dies. The NVA soldiers were only a few yards away from us.

Just then, the lieutenant called back, and asked us for a status update, and Murray, in a very soft voice, told him it looked like they were getting ready to make camp -- *right next to us*!

Several NVA soldiers had moved their gear very near where we were at, within about 10 yards of where we were hiding. I had eye contact with Murray, and I pointed to the radio, making a sign like a knife across the throat, which meant, "Shut it off!" Murray knew exactly what I was thinking; the slightest noise now, especially a radio squelch sound, would be unmistakable and give us away. He whispered into the phone, "We're going radio silent." and I reached over and turned the power off. We didn't have contact with the platoon for another 13 hours.[60]

To say that those were the most difficult hours, minutes, and seconds of my life would be a huge understatement. Four Marines, sitting in absolute silence, not moving a muscle for fear of a branch breaking or of letting out with an involuntary sneeze or a cough. Any sound at all would have given us away to the nearest NVA soldiers, and hence the rest of the NVA company, who were now resting and relaxing just a few yards from us.

We could hear them talking to each other, sometimes laughing, sometimes just low muffled exchanges. What worried me the most was when they stopped talking, and everything went dead silent, because I could imagine what that silence was like. Your ears never shut down completely. In the jungle, during wartime, they are always half awake, and if any of us had made the slightest sound or

---

[60] The Command Chronology report stated that we called in at 0200, but that's not correct. We went radio silent much earlier than that, and did not try to communicate again until the NVA had started to move out.

mistake, they would have heard us.

Every kind of possibility was going through my head. I couldn't help but imagine that one of us was going to screw up. I started to think about what could happen in that case. Our backs were, quite literally, against a wall. We would have to come out one side or the other of the bush, and we'd have to come out shooting. It was not going to end well for us. And then I started thinking, "What would happen if we were taken prisoner"? I suspect that same thought was going through everyone's mind because of something we had just learned a few days earlier ....

One of Our Own, Captured and Executed

[*What was going through our minds was what we had learned about the fate of one of our men who was captured. I am inserting this short narrative here to tell his story, and to explain why being captured was particularly on our minds right at the moment that we were surrounded and had gone into radio silence.*

Before I started carrying the radio for Lt. Manzi, his previous radio operator was L/Cpl. William Roland Prewitt. He had been with the platoon since they were first formed a year ago. He was well liked, and he did a great job while he was with us.

But there came a time when he started to become a bit paranoid about carrying the radio out in the field. He had seen almost all the original radiomen killed or wounded up to that point. His paranoia reached such a level that he finally asked to be transferred to another outfit. He was sent to one of the CAC (Combined Action Company groups) in our area, near Phu Bai.

We had just heard, before coming out into the field for this mission, that he had been wounded and captured by the Viet Cong. The rumors were that the VC had been parading him through some of the villages in the Phu Loc area, and that he had finally been executed (beheaded) on the steps of one of the village churches as an example. (Note: For many years, Prewitt was listed as MIA/POW. But in 1993, testimony from a former VC officer confirmed that the story was true; he had been killed on the steps of that church.

(Note: For many years, Prewitt was listed as MIA/POW. But in 1993, testimony from a former VC officer confirmed that the story was true; he had been killed and executed on the steps of that church.)[61]

(Surrounded by NVA, continued...)

The hours passed and somehow we were not detected. About 7:00 am in the morning, we could hear a lot of activity again, but the three NVA soldiers in front of our bush were still in place. Once again, we could hear the three of them talking. Then, after another couple of hours, we heard them moving back to the trail as the main group reformed. The four of us on the LP were physically and emotionally exhausted, and I was still very worried that one of us was going to slipup.

Finally, we heard them moving out. We waited another few minutes, just to make sure, and then Murray gave me a nod, and I turned the radio back on. We called Mike 3-3 to let them know. You could almost hear the sigh of relief on the other end. We were told to stay in place, and about a half hour later, our platoon caught up with us. To this day, I still can't imagine how we all were able to keep silent and not move for so long a period of time. It was a miracle.

But there was more to the story I did not know at the time. Last year I had the great privilege of having my old squad leader, Rhett Holley, and his wife Anne, visit for a few days. Rhett and I had a chance to finally sit down and catch up after 47 years. One of things I asked him about was what transpired that night while they were waiting to hear us call back.

Rhett said that battalion headquarters was very excited when they heard that there was an entire company of NVA bivouacked for the night, and that they had their exact coordinates, the coordinates of

---

[61] I am sorry for the pain that the retelling of this story might cause to the family of L/Cpl. Prewitt; he was a good Marine. But the rumor of what had happened to him was very much on our minds that night. We could only foresee two possible outcomes; either being captured or being killed.

our LP. An artillery strike would have yielded a very large body count. Rhett said that there was some discussion about it, back and forth, until Lt. Manzi let battalion HQ know that if they did call in artillery, and killed four of his Marines, he would personally see to it that "there would be hell to pay." That threat from Lt. Manzi may have been all that saved us. We'll never know, but now, after all these years, it sent a chill down my back, knowing that battalion headquarters had even considered it.

The Significance of that Event

All the details of our encounter with the NVA from the night before: troop size, the signs of hauling heavy equipment, direction of travel, etc., had been passed on to the logistics and intelligence units. In the last few months the NVA had been increasing its forces around the Marine base at Khe Sanh, but it was difficult to determine the level and extent that this was taking place. The majority of trails in the more mountainous area were concealed by tree canopies that were sometimes 60 feet high, and on the ground level, by tall elephant grass and bamboo thickets. Excellent country for concealment from aircraft above and from ground observation below. Visibility could be limited to no more than 5 meters.

Hills 881 North, 881 South and Hill 861 all provided a natural approach along their ridgelines from the western border of Laos, where NVA troops and supplies could detour off of the Ho Chi Minh trail, and head towards Khe Sanh. The spring of '67 had seen extremely fierce fighting around these hills, and that continued well into the early summer, when my battalion assumed the perimeter defense at Khe Sanh.

Although we may have not have realized it at the time, G2 Intelligence was now beginning to see a consistent buildup of troops and armaments being placed around the base, which would eventually lead to the 77-day Siege of Khe Sanh at the beginning of 1968.

Khe Sanh and surrounding hills. Note that the NVA (and our listening post were both inside the border of Laos.

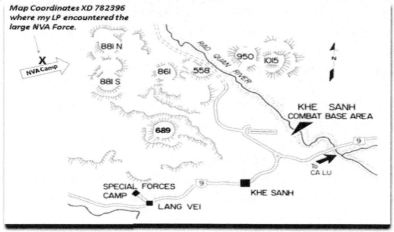

R&R in Taipei, Taiwan

I had been in-country for more than six months now, and the Lieutenant informed me that I had to take R&R (Rest and Recuperation Leave). It seemed that all the good destination spots (Hong Kong, Honolulu, Australia, etc.) had already been filled. That only left Taipei, Taiwan.

I wasn't very keen on the idea of going to Taipei, but the Lieutenant said I really had no choice. I was able to draw my monthly pay in advance, a little less than $140 (And that included combat pay!). There was a minimum amount of money you had to have in hand before you were allowed to leave, and I recall the Lieutenant ended up loaning me another $80.

The morning came for me to leave. I went up to our company headquarters hut, and was relieved to find that there was a corporal from H&S Company who was also going. That was good, because I had no idea how I was supposed to get to Taiwan from Khe Sanh.

The first order of business was to find our way to the airstrip (Blue Sector), and find a helicopter going south. It wasn't long before we had our opportunity to board a chopper going to Phu Bai, and from there, it was just matter of hanging around their airstrip until we found another one going south. We figured if they were offloading supplies, we would run over, help them unload, and then see if they would take us to Danang.

Our luck held, and the very next chopper was offloading personnel and heading south. We hitched a ride with him. I'd been on a lot of chopper rides, and it usually made me nervous, because sniper bullets could go right through the walls or up through the floor. This time, however, I felt that because I was going on a vacation, I would be immune to all that. It's strange sometimes how the mind works.

Once we had checked in at the R&R registration desk in Danang, we were told that there was a Braniff jet loading in an hour, and the destination was Taipei.

Then things took a turn. While waiting in the boarding area, I was struck with the worst toothache I had ever experienced. A pre-molar on the top left side of my mouth felt like it was being stabbed with a knife. The pain was so bad, I had to let my new-found buddy go on without me while I found a dentist. Luckily, we were in Danang, and there was a Navy dentist who was able to work on it. I ended up getting a large, temporary filling. I can remember the dentist telling me that it was only "a temporary." and I would need to get it replaced sometime in the near future. That filling lasted for nearly 25 years.

Since I had to stay in Danang overnight, I was assigned a temporary billet, and the next day I boarded another Braniff jet heading to Taipei. Except for a large contingent of Army guys who were heading there, I was by myself. When we finally arrived, there was a bus at the airport tarmac which picked us up, and we were driven to a USO (United Service Organization) in Taipei. Surprisingly, very few of the Army guys went into the USO; it seemed they already knew where they wanted to go. They hailed taxis and were off before I even had a chance to ask them where they were staying. There I was, by myself again. I walked dejectedly into the USO building, where I saw several service counters. You could get free coffee or order an inexpensive lunch. They even had their own bowling alley. Since I wasn't sure who to talk to, and also feeling a little depressed, I sat down at a long folding table and tried to figure out my next move. I knew I was going to have to find some place to stay, but the few places that I had heard about on the way from the airport didn't sound like they were anywhere I wanted to be by myself. This was also the first time I'd ever been in a large city, and Taipei was huge.

Except for the little English that the taxis drivers spoke, the only place I was going to find someone to talk to was right here. Sitting there, I happened to glance down at the table in front of me, and I saw that there was a small, metal nameplate underneath the table top. As I looked closer, I couldn't believe what I was seeing. It read, "*Monroe Table Company, Colfax, Iowa.*" What were the odds of something like that happening? The Monroe Company was just four blocks from my home back in Colfax. This was a sign, and it cheered me up quite a bit.

I finally found someone there at the USO who was able to give me some really good information about the best place to stay, how much it would cost, and where to go for meals. I also picked up some really handy tips. For instance, they had both cabs and rickshaws available in Taipei, but I was told, always take a cab because of the big "taxi cab/rickshaw war" going on at that time. It seems the cabs were winning (duh!!), so it wasn't worth it just to save a few bucks on a rickshaw ride only to get run over by a taxi.

Another question I had was about their currency. I can't remember if I had my American dollars converted to the new TWD (Taiwan Dollars) in Danang, or if it was at the airport in Taipei. I had $220 to start with, and I now had a big wad of TWD bills. The lady at the USO told me the going rate of exchange was about 40 to 1, so my $220 was now $8800 in TWD's.

The hotel I was going to stay at was called "The President," and it was supposed to be the nicest hotel in the city. I was only going to be there three nights now, since I'd used up a day of my R&R already getting my tooth fixed. She told me the rooms were $400 TWD a night, which was like $10 (American). That meant it was only going to be $30 U.S, which was $1200 TWD. She also told me it should never cost more than $100 TWD to take a cab anywhere in the city.

I was a little skeptical about "how nice" a hotel might be for just $10 (American) per night, but when I got there, it was really very classy. I obviously wasn't going to be seeing any of the Army guys here, because, if you brought a "guest" in with you, you had to register them with the front desk clerk each time they came in This was practice that was probably designed to make them, and their "guests," a little nervous, and hence, I assumed most of the Army guys were finding digs in the lower class part of town.

When I was at the USO the next day, I asked if there were any movie theaters, and was told my best bet was an outdoor theater near the city park. I was feeling pretty daring by now, so I just gave the cab driver the name of the park, and he drove me straight to it. It looked like most of the people were walking towards the opposite end from where I was so I just followed everyone through an entrance way. I was surprised to see that there was no one charge for tickets. It was evidently free to the public. It was a pretty straightforward setup. No concession stands, just a series of bleachers in a semicircle around a large, outdoor screen.

The seats were like stadium bleachers back home at a high school football game. I had come early enough that I didn't have any problem finding somewhere to sit. I had hoped I might see some other Americans there. At the very least, I was sure I'd see some servicemen, because they were coming in almost daily from Vietnam. But by the time the movie started, I still had not seen any Americans. All I remember about the movie was that it was an American Western, and the audio track was in English, with Chinese subtitles. I couldn't believe it!

When the movie was over, it took me a lot longer to get out than it did to get in. My next challenge was to get back to the street and find a taxi. The only problem was there were no taxis in that part of town at that time of night. I waited for over an hour, and then started thinking about walking back to the hotel, but I wasn't sure which way to go. I hadn't really paid that much attention on the way down there, and now I was really screwed.

I turned and walked back into the park where it was more lighted, and sat down on a park bench, hoping someone who could speak English might come along, but I didn't see anyone, not even a policeman.

Luckily, the night air wasn't all that cold, but I had brought a jacket just in case. I rolled up the jacket and made a pillow out of it with the intention of just lying down for a little while. Then I'd get up and walk around the park some more. It was deserted.

Somewhere around 1 AM, I laid down, fell asleep, and didn't get back up until I was awakened by the sound of a man walking briskly past the bench. He was evidently out for his morning exercise. As I sat up and started to stretch, I turned to my right, and was startled to see a large group of older Chinese folks, all doing what looked to me like some sort of slow motion dance. They were all moving in time with each other, and the more I looked at it, the more it started to look like they were doing some kind of martial arts moves. I later found out it was a popular exercise called Tai Chi, but at the time, I had no idea what I was looking at.

No one seemed bothered at all by my presence. As a matter of fact, they all just acted like I wasn't there. They probably had seen a fair share of drunken sailors or Marines, and they may have thought I was just sleeping off a rowdy night on the town. I think they would have been even more shocked if they knew that this was my idea of "a rowdy night on the town."

The good news was that the taxis were now up and running again, and all I had to tell the driver was "*The President Hotel*." and he took me right back there. I was starting to like this place. I'd found that the best place for breakfast and lunch was at the USO. The best place for supper, however, was a well-known supper club that had been recommended to me. It was called "Eddies."

I imagine some enterprising Chinese restaurateur had realized that if he wanted to tap into the large flow of Americans (both tourists and military servicemen), he needed to set up a nice steak house with American music, American beer and drinks, a familiar American ambience, and with good service. And that is exactly what he had done. I loved "Eddies." If it were here in the states, I'd still be going to it.

This was now my second night here at Eddies, and already I was starting to develop a crush on my waitress. Of course, she didn't speak (or didn't want to speak) English, and I didn't know any Chinese, so it didn't really matter. Besides, if she did speak English, I wouldn't have known what to say. I was just a 19-year old, small town, Iowa boy, fresh from the sticks, and I was just happy that I was making my way around this strange, exotic city without any problems. It made me feel like a seasoned, world traveler, but truth be told, I was really just happy that I was here now, and not back in Vietnam.

When the next morning came, it was time to depart for the airport. I was sorry to leave all these comforts, but also eager to get back to my unit. It might seem strange, but I was starting to feel that I was part of something back there. I'd finally made the commitment to extend for an additional 6 months in Vietnam. This would allow me to take a 30-day leave back home in the States before I started the next part of my tour. Who knew, maybe the war would be over before I had to come back.

As I walked down to check out of the hotel, I noticed the young man who had been responsible for making sure my room got cleaned and straightened every day. He also took care of any laundry needs, and would dutifully return any change I might have left in my pockets from the night before. The change and small bills were always stacked neatly on the night stand when I came back to my room in the afternoon.

The young man followed me out the door and hailed a cab for me. I gave the driver my two small carrying bags and asked him how much for the ride to the airport. Then I gave him double that amount so as to take care of his tip.

At the very last moment, I realized I still had quite a bit of money left, so I dug it all out of my wallet, and took out all the change from my pocket, and handed it to the room boy. I didn't get the reaction I was expecting. He tried to give it back to me and shook his head, but I eventually prevailed, and he took it. Then, he started crying.

That's the signal I was looking for! That meant he wasn't insulted by the amount I'd given him. So, with that all taken care of, I jumped into the cab and went off to the airport. On the flight back, I was talking to one American, and I told him I gave the room boy about $2000 TWD, which was about $50 American, and he told me that was probably two month's wages for him. Good, I thought; I wasn't going to need it where I was going anyway.

It didn't dawn on me until I finally got back with my unit at Khe Sanh that I stilled owed the Lieutenant for the $80 he had loaned me. I wasn't sorry that I had given the room boy that big of a tip, but it now meant I was going to have to wait for the next payday to be able to pay him back. When I mentioned it to him, Lt. Manzi just said, "Don't worry about it, the guys all pitched in to come up with that money." And then he added, with a little bit of a laugh, "They all thought it would be worth it to get rid of you for a week." I always knew that he was making that last part up. I was still sure that the $80 came from him and not from a collection he had taken up.

Thinking About My Future in the Marine Corps

The Lieutenant was a "tough cookie." and not an easy man to get to know. And, although I was his radioman and we were together almost constantly out in the field, I would never think of addressing him any other way than, "Lieutenant." or "Sir."

He had a more familiar relationship with his NCO's, especially Sgt. Holley, but the squad leaders were more like his foreman, making sure that the "grunts" (we enlisted men) properly carried out his orders. I felt good about the fact that he never seemed to feel that he had to yell at me, and he never questioned any of the answers I would give him when he asked something. I think the only time he expressed concern was when I told him I was going to sign up for a 6-month extension in Vietnam.

About that, the Lieutenant suggested that a better plan would be for me to just finish my current tour. Once I was back stateside, I should apply for NCO school. Then he said something that really changed my thinking. He said, "Personally, I'd like to see you apply for OCS (Officers Candidate School) when you start to get close to the end of your enlistment."

Afterwards, I thought about that. I thought about it a lot. I had never envisioned myself becoming an officer. It wasn't because I disliked being in the Marine Corps, I actually did. I liked the fact that everything boiled down to the fact that you were given an order (or a mission) and then you did it. No making excuses, no whining, you just did it. And if one approach didn't work, then you tried something else until it was completed. I had learned early on that that the Marine Corps could be unforgiving about failure, but they gave "extra points" for showing initiative.

3/26 is Awarded the "Presidential Unit Citation"

After I came back from R&R, I learned that our unit, 3rd Battalion, 26th Marine Regiment, was being awarded the Presidential Unit Citation. This was quite an honor as our unit, which had only been activated for a little more than a year, and had only been in Vietnam for 9 months.

Since I wasn't part of the original unit when it landed, I was unaware of 3/26's previous history. I learned later that they were first activated during WWII, specifically to be part of the Pacific Campaign. I also learned that they had been awarded their first Presidential Unit Citation during the assault on Iwo Jima. It was the largest Marine assault force ever assembled, and was comprised of 3 Divisions of Marines. Over 7,000 Marines were killed on Iwo Jima, and another 20,000 were wounded.

The Criteria for the Presidential Unit Citation is as follows:

*It is conferred on units of the armed forces of the United States and of cobelligerent nations, for extraordinary heroism in action against an armed enemy. The unit must display such gallantry, determination, and esprit de corps in accomplishing its mission as to set it apart from **and above all other units participating in the same campaign**. The degree of heroism required is the same that which would warrant award of the Navy Cross to an individual.*

Four months later, at the beginning of 1968 and the start of the Tet Offensive, 3/26 would earn a 3rd Presidential Unit Citation during the 77-day siege of Khe Sanh. Khe Sanh would become one of the most publicized and pivotal events in the entire Vietnam War, with coverage in all the newspapers, and almost daily television feeds being sent to news stations around the world.

Our Last Week at Khe Sanh

It was now late August of 1967. Our unit was still at Khe Sanh, but it was general knowledge that we would soon be moving even further north to an artillery combat base named "Con Thien."

Our field missions had taken on a familiar strategy that had worked well for us in the past.

It was called "Prep-Insertion-Ambush"[62], and here is how it worked. A Marine battalion will commonly send out specialized Recon units to quietly assess enemy activity (This was the kind of unit I was originally supposed to be assigned to.). First, there would be some artillery softening up of the area, then a Recon[63] team was inserted by helicopter. The Recon team would move out and reconnoiter for anywhere from several days up to a week before returning to base. We would use the information they gathered to help plan sweep and ambush missions. The Recon teams were small groups of specially trained Marines, usually 6 or less, and it was an extremely dangerous profession to be in

Most recently, our Recon teams had been having a lot of unplanned encounters with the bad guys. It seems that the NVA had picked up on our strategies, and were trying to intercept our teams at the point of insertion, with much larger, platoon or even company-sized forces.

This offered us a very tantalizing opportunity. We would send a rifle company out on foot ahead of time. They would quietly make their way to the planned insertion sites, set up in ambush, and then a fake Recon team would be inserted in. It started out as a game of cat and mouse that the NVA were playing, and then we changed the rules and added a second, bigger cat to the game. It usually worked out pretty well.

On September 2nd, Mike Company was marching to a point about 12 klicks (about 7.5 miles) out from Khe Sanh to play the "*fake insertion game.*" which was to take place the next day. This was not

---

[62] "Prep-Insertion-Ambush" – "Prep" refers to an initial artillery bombardment that would take place. Right behind that would come a single, low-flying helicopter, with a single 6-man or 7-man "Recon" unit. A Marine rifle company would be sent to the area well before, and would be lying in ambush, all around the insertion point, waiting for any enemy troops. The artillery preparation would be the key to getting their attention, and draw them towards the area where we had set the ambushes.

achieved without some considerable effort. Although the thick jungle and double and triple-canopied trees allowed us to move undetected, at the same time, it made out progress more difficult. There were few or no watering points along the way. With high temperatures, a staggering heat index, and heavy field gear, heat casualties became a major concern. Still, we humped all night, and were able to get set up in an ideal location by about 0100 (1AM in the morning). Our bait, the Recon team insertion, was set for 1000 (10AM), so we planned to just sit and wait for everything to play out.

As happened many times, the plans were changed. A half hour after we got to our predetermined location, a call came from battalion headquarters telling us the mission was scrubbed, and we had to immediately start humping back to a point on Hwy 9, where we would be picked up by truck convoy and taken back to Khe Sanh. This made everyone very unhappy after all the effort we had put in, and we suffered more than a few heat casualties on our 8-hour trek back to the pickup point.

We took a different route on our way back, and I can remember at one point we did have to cross a rather imposing little stream. Once we got on the other side, the only way forward was directly up an almost vertical rock face, about 30 feet high, with water cascading just to our left from a
waterfall. The only thing to grasp onto were slippery rock edges and roots and vines that were on the cliff face.

It was still pitch dark, and we were trying to move as silently as possible. I remember thinking that it was impossible with so many men and such heavy gear, but about two thirds of the way up, with each Marine grabbing the last handhold that the previous one in front of them had, I could see that we were not only doing it, but were going to do it without a lot of difficulty. Even though I was carrying an extra heavy load, with my radio and gear, and some others carrying cumbersome ammunition boxes, heavy machines guns, etc., it still went quite smoothly. It seemed amazing to me, and to this day, I think back to that moment and wonder how in the hell we were able to do it, climbing nearly 3 stories straight up the side of a slippery waterfall in total darkness.

We finally made it to the pickup point in the early afternoon, and the convoy was there waiting for us. The trip back to Khe Sanh was uneventful, and finally we had a chance to rest. We spent all of the next day writing letters, making sure our weapons were in order, drawing supplies, and getting our gear ready to "get the hell out of Dodge" and head directly into new territory.

The following morning, we were flown by helicopter to Camp Carroll, where we met up with the rest of the Battalion and we bivouacked there for the night. The next morning, September 7th, we loaded onto trucks for the ride north towards Con Thien, driving along the MSR (main supply route) which was the only road in and out.

Con Thien: A Very Dangerous Place

Most of us were feeling a mixture of confidence and apprehension about this move to the forward base at Con Thien. For one thing, it was the Marines' most forward combat base, only a couple of miles from the DMZ, and perilously close to the Laotian border, which was the gateway for the NVA infiltration into the south. Still, in our minds, we continued to feel a high degree of confidence in our own abilities and experience. We felt it wasn't going to be a whole lot different from what we had already experienced at Khe Sanh.

We were wrong. In the next six days, our entire Battalion would suffer nearly 40% casualties. In the following weeks during September, that number would climb to nearly 50%, making September of 1967 the deadliest month in the Battalion's long history.

In the last four years I've had the opportunity to read and learn a great deal more about what we were walking into. None of us had any idea at the time, not even our field officers. The two deadliest elements that we were going to deal with were, one, the massive NVA artillery coming from just across the DMZ, and two, the NVA soldier himself, this time in very large numbers.[64]

The NVA Artillery Zone

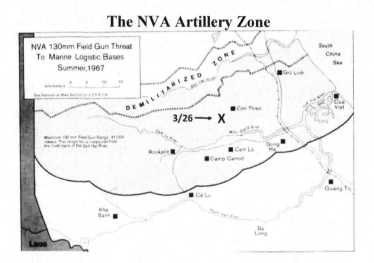

NVA Artillery – Soviet Supplied and Soviet Trained

The Soviet tactic -- which the North Vietnamese followed -- was to position their heavy artillery pieces just beyond the range of U.S. 105mm and 155mm artillery, which were the most common guns in the U.S. artillery arsenal, which had 10,500 and 14,800 meter ranges, respectively.

The Soviet 152mm guns had a range of 14,955 meters, while their 130mm artillery piece could shoot 31,000 meters (about 19 miles). They also had 140mm rockets. That meant that the NVA could fire on most American artillery bases, and field troops, with little threat from effective return fire.

---

[64] It was determined later that between September 7th and September 10th, we were directly engaged with an entire NVA Regiment, the 812th NVA Regiment, about 3000 men strong. On the first day of battle, we had only 3 companies in the field, about 700 men.

Besides the 152 mm and 130mm artillery pieces and 140mm rockets, the NVA were provided some of the finest artillery training by both Russian and Chinese advisors. The NVA artillery positions were virtually untouchable except by artillery counterbattery fire or aerial interdiction, and at this point in the war, the U.S. was still not bombing into the DMZ. The area we were moving into was one where the NVA had virtually dictated the nature of the battles that took place.

It was a common belief amongst our troops that, although the NVA soldier was a battle hardened and worthy opponent, they were not as well trained as we were, and that their fierceness in battle was only due to being "doped up" prior to going into battle. Nothing could be further from the truth. The typical NVA soldier went through a training process very similar to our own. Along with the formal military training, there was an equal counterpart of ideological training as well. In fact, every NVA unit had embedded political cadres that accompanied them. These cadres monitored and evaluated performance all the way down to the 3-man cells that were the backbone of every NVA unit. Drug use was almost non-existent among NVA troops.[65]

The Set-Piece Strategy: Old Theory, Wrong War

The "Set-Piece Strategy." the brain child of Robert McNamara and fully endorsed by General Westmoreland, was that you can set up forward combat bases like Khe Sanh and Con Thien, right on the front doorstep of North Vietnam. When those bases are attacked directly, they can be held by the defending forces, while the enemy outside the gates will be bombed out of existence by our superior air support. In chess, it's like presenting a pawn or some other insignificant piece to trigger an attack.

---

[65] An excellent, and eye-opening look at what life was like for the typical NVA soldier can be found in the seminal work done by Lanning and Cragg in the book, "Inside the VC and the NVA", Fawcett Columbine Ballantine Books.

Unfortunately, up to this point, the NVA generals were too smart to fall for that, so the U.S. generals had taken to sending units (like ours) out to sweep the areas around Con Thien, to see if they could draw the enemy out in large numbers. Just a few months prior, one of the battalions we were to be replacing had done a similar sweep in the same area and had encountered a large force of NVA. There were significant casualties on both sides. Now, it looked like we were being sent out into similar situation.

The problem was, we were never informed of the plan. We were told that this would be a normal sweep of the area before taking up positions on the perimeter line of Con Thien. We were told to only expect "light activity."

All the original members in my Battalion were due to rotate back to the states sometime in late October. After this initial sweep, we were to take over responsibility for perimeter defense. Typically, that assignment would last one month, and then another Battalion would take our place and we would presumably be moving back to Dong Ha. From there, the original members of our Battalion would be rotating back home, their 13-month Vietnam tour would be over.

Unfortunately, plans change. We were about to engage in a 4-day, life and death struggle with the 812th NVA Regiment, 3000 men strong and supplemented by heavy weapons companies, special Sapper platoons, and a deadly concentration of NVA artillery and rocket fire from just across the DMZ.

Chapter 9

Con Thien: The Hill of Angels

The truck transport ride was uneventful. The morning was overcast with low cloud cover and it would remain this way, on and off, for the next several days. I was actually feeling pretty comfortable riding in the back of the 6X6 truck, using my radio and pack as a back rest. I pulled out a letter that I'd received from my Mom, I wanted to reread certain parts of it that I'd just glanced at before.

Mom had written to me that one of my friends from high school, Dennis Conn, was in the Marines and was currently stationed at Dong Ha. Our truck was just going over a high rise in the road and you could see out for miles in 3 directions. I yelled over and asked Sgt. Holley where Dong Ha was located from here, and he pointed off to the southeast, towards a high point on the landscape and said, "There it is. Why, you got plans for the weekend?" I wanted to laugh, but I was suddenly overcome with a tremendous feeling of homesickness and I wished more than anything I could somehow get over there and just say "Hello" to Dennis. Ever since my return from R&R in Taipei a few weeks ago, I had been thinking about home a lot, and I had made the commitment to extend my tour in Vietnam for another 6 months in exchange for a 30-day leave back to the states. That would be 30 days back in Colfax, not in some foreign place like Taiwan where I'd just come back from. Just another month or so and we'd be finished with our duty rotation at Con Thien. It was very comforting to think that I might be able to go back home soon. Now I had something to look forward to. Something to dream about.

September 7, 1967: The Churchyard

We were just about 3 miles north of Cam Lo when we reached our debarking point. Once we were off the trucks, and Mike Company was assembled on the ground, we started to make our way west, towards an old, abandoned church where we would establish a

Battalion perimeter.[66] Once that was done, each company would send out patrols in front of their positions and then they would return to their lines. The terrain south of the Churchyard was a series of rice paddies, demarcated by tree lines which were made up into little squares. West of there, the land was characterized by bushes, low scrub, and lots of trees. It was easy to see how a large group of enemy soldiers could go completely undetected in such a landscape.

It was about midday when we started to hear a lot of activity over the radio. India Company had made contact with a group of NVA of unknown size. There was no other information. Our 3rd platoon was spread out on a flat piece of ground with low brush and scrub. Suddenly, we started to take incoming small arms fire from directly in front of us. There was a tree line behind us, maybe 100 yards or so. At first it was just a "pop." "pop." "pop." and then, when our guys started firing back, it became a continuous, rising string of single and automatic weapon fire from both sides.

We were in a bad position We were out in the open and on flat ground. The enemy, half hidden in the scrub brush, was moving towards us. It was impossible to tell how many of them there were, but from the volume of incoming fire, we knew it was a substantially-sized group, possibly a full company. Lt. Manzi yelled to both squads on either side of him, "Dig in!." "Dig In!" This meant that we were going to make a stand right there.

I frantically pulled off my pack and radio and struggled to get my e-tool[67] out. The Lieutenant was down on one knee now, firing his M-16. I had to fight the urge to grab my M-16 and start firing back too. At any moment we would likely be hit with incoming mortar shells and the scrub plants provided no protection, just concealment. If we were going to hold this position, we would have to have a hole to

---

[66] The 1st Battalion, 9th Marines had been in this area several weeks earlier. There were already some fighting holes dug around the old churchyard. We widened and dug some of them a little deeper, they were already starting to cave in.

[67] An e-tool is an "entrenching tool", or shovel, which folds up and is carried on your backpack.

fight from. I could see other Marines down the line doing the same; one person firing, one person digging. It took a tremendous amount of discipline to focus on digging a hole with bullets whizzing around everywhere, but we had been in these situations before, and everyone knew what they had to do.

I took my e-tool and plunged it into the ground, expecting to feel the soft earth give way, like the soil we were used to back at Khe Sanh, but this was like hardened brick clay, baked in the sun. I swung it again at the ground and this time the force of the contact came back through my arms and down my spine, creating what felt like an electric shock and one of the greatest pains I had ever felt in my life. The pain was so severe, my body jerked up and I let out a terrible scream.[68] As I was straightening up, I bumped my right shoulder against the Lieutenant's left shoulder … just as a round from an AK-47 went right between us! We could both feel the force of the bullet when it grazed our shirts. I looked at my shirt sleeve, then at the Lieutenant. He was staring at me with the same sense of disbelief, then, turning back forwards again, he started firing his M-16 in earnest. I once again picked up the shovel. The earth was coming out now in large, heavy clumps and I soon had a hole that we could both just barely fit in. It would have to do.

I reached for my M-16. The shovel was laying on top of it, and as I grabbed it by the blade, it felt red hot. Now that I was back in the fight. I quickly looked around for Doc O'Connell. Doc usually stayed near the Lieutenant and I but he was off somewhere with either the 1st or 3rd squad, most likely tending one of the wounded. As I looked to my right, I saw an NVA soldier drop dead about 5 yards in front of Sgt. Holley's position.

If you had ever seen the sheer volume of fire power that is put out by

---

[68] Normally, I would have expected that the force of the blow, and the resulting shock wave going down my spinal cord, would have resulted in a painful back injury that would have taken at least a week to heal, but I don't remember having a problem with my back after that incident. I've always assumed it was because I had all that adrenaline coursing through my body at that moment (and over the next few days).

a Marine rifle platoon, you might wonder how anything could survive in front of that, but now, it seemed like every time one NVA soldier would go down, two more would pop back up to take his place. When we started seeing the green, .50 caliber tracer rounds shooting past us, we knew for sure that this had to be a large, company-sized force.

The Lieutenant picked up the radio handset and called our Company Commander to give him our status. We had several casualties, but no KIA's as of yet. Captain DeBona told us to withdraw the platoon back towards the tree line, and then make our way to the Churchyard[69] where the rest of Mike Company was defending our perimeter line.

Lt. Manzi called out to have our 1st and 3rd squads (the 2 squads our left and right) to retreat with their wounded back the way we had come. After both squads had made their way back to the tree line, the Lieutenant sent the 2nd squad back (the squad that he and I were embedded with). The Lieutenant and I provided covering fire for them as they moved back.

I had been assuming that the Lieutenant and I would retreat with the 2nd squad, but they were nearly back to the tree line by now. I was more than a little concerned with the fact that we were now the only ones out there, but finally the Lieutenant jumped up out of the hole, grabbed me by the shoulder and hauled me out, pack, radio and all. We both quickly made our way back towards the questionable safety of the tree line, while the other 3 squads now gave us covering fire. It's hard to describe the sight of running back towards, and into, the volley of covering fire now being laid down by our 3 squads. You could actually hear rounds whizzing past your ears from both directions and see the red tracer rounds coming from our 2 M-60

---

[69] "The Churchyard" was an abandoned (Catholic) church, located a short way off the Main Supply Route road that led to Con Thien. It was also supposed to be a starting point where we were going to begin our original sweep of the valley around the Con Thien fire base.

machine guns, and then see the occasional green tracer rounds flying towards the tree line from the NVA heavy machine guns. That's a sight that not too many people will ever get to see. Once we made it back, the Lieutenant double timed our platoon back towards the Churchyard.

By now, Kilo Company had moved to support India Company, and all our tanks (3 gunner tanks and a flame tank) moved with them. The tanks became stalled in the grid work of dikes and rice paddies before they could reach India Company.

By the time my platoon got back and was positioned in the new perimeter, it was late afternoon. There were fighting holes that had already been dug, and in other spots we either started digging new ones, or in some cases, used holes that had been dug out by bombs or artillery from previous engagements that took place in the early summer. There was a line of trees behind us, and the Mike Company Command post and our 60mm mortar team was just behind that.

About 1720 (5:20 PM), we could hear, off to our left, sporadic 175mm and 130mm NVA artillery fire coming in from just across the DMZ. The enemy's targeting was very accurate. They already had this area zeroed in for some time, and now that we were in close combat, the enemy forward observers could give their artillery teams exact coordinates. It wasn't long before the tree line to the front my platoon started erupting with automatic weapons fire and we again found ourselves in direct contact with what seemed to be several companies of NVA soldiers probing out part of the perimeter line.

Then came more incoming NVA mortar fire, and just to ratchet up our nerves even further, we started getting sporadic, 140 mm[70] rocket fire landing in front of and behind us. The blasts were deafening, and the fire and black smoke made us all squirm down as far into our fighting holes as we could possibly get. It was like a

---

[70] The 175mm and 130mm NVA artillery and the 140mm rocket were all being fired from just across the DMZ. The mortar fire (61mm and 82mm NVA mortars) were coming from the NVA units we were engaged with.

game of "whack-a-mole." and we were the moles. If you can imagine volcanos, earthquakes, and the worst thunderstorm you've ever been in, all erupting at once, you can start to get an idea what that is like. All you could do was keep your head down, it was like the end of the world. Even the enemy advance halted as they made themselves as flat as they could on the open ground.

When the artillery and rockets finally stopped, the fire fights took up again in earnest. I had the radio lying between the Lieutenant and myself, with the volume all the way up so I would have my hands free to fire my M-16 and use both hands to change out spent magazines, or reload from the extra ammo I had in my pack. I was starting to worry about running out, I had only brought about 200 rounds into the field with me this time, and I had chosen to leave my .45 behind. I had been expecting just 2 days in the field before we were to take over our new positions at Con Thien.

It was about this time that I stood up in our fighting hole to take a better shot at a new, heavy gun position that was in front of us. I can remember firing off 3 more rounds, and then having to change magazines. I reached down to pull one out of my side pocket. when a large, .51 caliber round whizzed just above my right ear. I swear I could see it coming and the compression of the air, due to being so close to my face, smacked me down. I thought I'd been hit, and my right eye ached like I'd been punched in the face.

At this point, the Lieutenant became greatly concerned about what was happening with the 3rd squad, which was tied into the perimeter on our right. We'd been trying to raise them on the radio, but with all the noise and bedlam going on over the net, we couldn't tell what was happening.

It was at that point that the Lieutenant decided he had to see what was happening over there. He slapped me on the shoulder and jumped up out of the hole and was quickly moving down just behind the other fighting holes on our line. I grabbed the shoulder strap of my pack/radio and hauled my butt out, just a few steps behind him, but as I was struggling to get the radio on I had fallen a little further behind and I was worried about losing sight of him. Suddenly, there was an explosion in front of me and I was blown right off my feet. My helmet, my glasses, my rifle, and my pack all went flying through the air with me and when I landed on the ground I could feel an intense, burning pain, just below my left knee and along my left side.

I was lying flat on my back. My ears were ringing and I felt like I was going to pass out, but I knew if I did, I wasn't going to wake up, so I started shouting just to keep myself awake. For some reason, I chose to shout my own name, "Ward!" "Ward!" "Ward!" It was like I was trying to give myself an order. Anything to just to keep myself conscious. I knew I had to get up, but I didn't know how much of my left leg was still there, so I rolled over onto my right side. I could see that my trousers were ripped where the shrapnel went through, and I could see that I was bleeding, but other than that, it seemed like my leg was there.

Now, I had to find my rifle, so I started crawling around, feeling for it as my head started to clear a bit. I found the radio and pack first, and my rifle was next to it. Next I found my helmet, but I never did find my glasses. This was a problem. I didn't have the best vision in the first place, but now it was almost impossible to see clearly. Also, I had become totally disorientated and I wasn't sure which direction to go.

As I started crawling, I could see and hear figures in front of me, about 40 feet away, and that was the direction I thought the Lieutenant had gone, but I wasn't sure of anything. I could also see green, Marine Corps uniforms and helmets, but, as my hearing was starting to come back, I was also hearing Vietnamese voices. I was starting to feel the panic come back and it quickly replaced the feeling of shock I had been experiencing.[71] What if these aren't Marines? I wouldn't be able to tell until they were right on top of me. Do I call out to them? Or, do I keep crawling until I find our lines? Which way do I crawl?

I kept crawling, but this time I went in the other direction. I was now sure that there were NVA in the direction I had been going. Finally, I heard someone calling my name. It sounded like Cpl. Szabo, but I never determined that for sure. I could stand on my feet now, and I limped along in a low, painful squat until I came to an empty fighting hole. It was bigger than the one I had been in before, but I jumped in anyway. I'd only been there for a few seconds when right behind me came Fossell and Szabo, two of our corporals. I started digging desperately through my pack. I'd remembered that I had an extra pair of glasses. I asked Cpl. Fossell, "Have you seen the Lieutenant?." and he replied, "The Lieutenant's dead." I just stared at him. Somehow, that didn't seem possible to me, and I asked him again, "Have you seen the Lieutenant?" When he repeated it again, it began to sink into my head. [72]

Cpl. Fossell, who was now temporarily in charge, called company headquarters to tell them and then informed the other squad leaders. The Captain instructed us to pull the platoon back towards the Churchyard where the command post was set up. Once again, our platoon was pulled back, but this time they evacuated the wounded and dead first. The final ones to pull back off the line were Sgt. Holley, Corporal Fossell, and Szabo. I went with them, but about

---

[71] One of the post traumatic experiences that I would continue to have for many years was to wake up in the middle of the night with "night terrors" and hear Vietnamese voices, always just out of sight. I finally learned to deal with it by just "talking back to them", and at one point, I even threatened to go learn Vietnamese, just so I would know what they were saying. Strangely, this seemed to shut them up for good. I don't think they wanted me to know what they were planning. (Sometimes you have to get a little crazy just to get over "being crazy".)

[72] Many years later, when I finally got back in touch with Rhett Holley, and we were talking about that incident, he recalled that I'd asked him the same question the next morning, "Had he seen the Lieutenant?" He thought, at the time, that I must have gotten separated the previous night and didn't know that the Lieutenant had been killed.

halfway back, the handset to my radio had fallen on the ground and as I moved forward, it got caught on a bush. I just leaned forward and kept pulling, figuring it would eventually come loose. It did, and when it did, the stretched out cord and handset flew past my head and in front of me, then it swung back and wrapped itself around my legs. I went down like a sack of potatoes and was just lying there, all trussed up on the ground like a calf in a rodeo. As I tried to unwrap the cord from around my legs, I thought to myself how bizarre this all was, like a Road Runner cartoon. I was desperately trying to keep the thought out of my mind that Lt. Manzi had been killed.

Later, we found out what had happened. When the 2nd platoon had been pulled out of the line to swing back and protect an opening in India Company's line, this left an empty hole in the larger perimeter line. Lt. Manzi was ordered to stretch out our 3rd platoon to make up the difference, but by then, more NVA were coming through the hole. When the Lieutenant got to the end of our platoon's line, he was immediately killed by small arms fire, likely by NVA dressed in Marine uniforms. A full platoon of NVA managed to get through and attacked our command post and our 81mm mortar teams before they were finally taken out. When we finally reorganized and tightened up our perimeter, the place where our old Command Post was now "No Man's Land." in front of our new front perimeter line.[73]

When I made it back to the wall where the old church stood, I wasn't sure at all where my platoon was at, they had been dispersed and repositioned along new perimeter lines. I think I must have been in or near where our new Command Post was now at. There were several people who were wounded, sitting and leaning against the church wall. There was a large pile of weapons, packs, canteens, and cartridge belts stacked off to the left of me. The gear was from the dead and the severely wounded, both NVA and Marines. This pile

---

[73] During that first direct attack, Mike Company alone had been hit by an estimated 60, 140mm rockets and 70, 82mm mortar rounds as well as an unknown amount of artillery rounds.

would be used later as we began to run low on ammunition or gear. I sat down against the wall and partially cut open my left trouser leg to see if I could assess the damage. The leg still hurt quite a bit and it was still bleeding, but I could see the edge of a piece of the shrapnel that had hit me sticking out through the skin. Every time I moved now, my pants leg would drag across exposed piece of shrapnel and the pain was excruciating. All I could think of to do was cut my pants leg completely off. While I was doing that, one of the corpsman came over to take a look. He was able to pull out the extruding piece out, but said it was likely there was still some in there. He bandaged it up and that was all he could do for me then.

I needed to find my platoon. It was dark now, and still a lot of people running around as the new perimeter lines were being filled in. I was standing next to the pile of weapons and cartridge belts when I saw a curious Marine pick up an NVA cartridge belt. It still had a Chicom grenade hooked to it. Just as he lifted it up, the grenade fell off and the pin popped. Everyone standing around ran or dove for cover. I only made it a few steps, then hit the ground and got as flat as I could. The grenade went off, but there was no shrapnel, and it sounded more like a big firecracker than a grenade. The detonator cap had gone off, but the rest of it was a dud. Everyone got up, shaken but glad to still be alive. We didn't need those kinds of things happening with everything else going on.

I found a staff sergeant and told him who I was with. He sent me down with another Marine to an open spot on the line. I didn't know this guy, and no one seemed know where 3rd platoon was at, so I spent the rest of the night there. Things were settling down about 2300 that night, but there still were occasional enemy probes. Everyone was on edge and I doubt that anyone got more than an hour or two of sleep. A few medevac helicopters managed to come in, but they were drawing a lot of fire, so evacuations were only for the most severely wounded. The walking wounded and the dead would have to wait.

My leg was swelling and throbbing a good bit, but I found if I kept it moving, it not only helped with the pain, but also to kept my mind focused. The guy in the fighting hole with me wasn't much of a talker, I don't even know what rank he was, although that didn't matter to me in the least. At one point we realized that we both were very low on ammunition. I think I had one magazine left, 3 empty magazines, and no more extra ammo in my pack. We decided he would go back to the CP area and try to get some more ammunition and I would stay in the hole until he got back. My biggest worry was that he was going to get shanghaied and put somewhere else along the line. I started counting what resources I had left. One magazine of ammo (16 rounds) and 1 grenade. That wouldn't last long if we had another assault in the early morning hours.

Normally, I would be more worried about my rifle ammunition, but in situations like tonight, when the enemy is probing the lines, and you hear something, we were taught to throw a grenade first rather than give away our position with a muzzle flash. Many times snipers will just wait for a muzzle flash to flush out a target. The problem with only having 1 grenade left was that I had a bit of a superstition about always keeping at least 1 grenade. I had a morbid fear of getting bayoneted if we were ever overrun. I wasn't afraid of getting in a fight, but I had nightmares about getting overrun by 2 or 3 NVA. In that case, I always kept a grenade in my front shirt pocket so that if that did happen, I could pull the pin, and have a little surprise for everyone. Like I said, it was kind of a morbid thought, but it gave me a little bit of comfort knowing that the little bastards weren't going to get away with it.

After about 30 minutes, my partner came back and he only had 8 boxes (20 rounds each) of ammunition. We each took 4 and started filling our empty magazines. I would normally only put 16 rounds in a magazine because I felt it made the chance of a jam less likely. This time I was filling them up and I had just pulled the one out of my rifle to reload it when I dropped it on the ground. It was very dark, and hard to see, so I felt around on the ground, found another magazine I had already reloaded and put it back in my rifle.

A little while later someone whispered from the next fighting hole that we would be having another medevac coming in soon, and they wanted us to fire a full clip each into the brush and tree line to our front. This was a strategy we would often do to keep any potential sniper's heads down while the chopper was coming in. We all got ready and when they gave the signal we all started firing into the darkness. Normally you can't see where the rounds are hitting, but this time all my shots were coming out like lasers. After I'd fired off several rounds, I realized I had really messed up and was firing all tracer rounds. In each ammunition box there is one 20-round carton of tracer bullets. Some people liked to put one or more tracers in their magazine so they could get an idea where they were shooting in the dark. We never used them that way, but when they were handing out the extra ammunition, no one had looked at the box and I had ended up filling one full magazine with all tracer rounds. It was almost impossible to tell how many other magazines I had put them into, so I just stopped firing, and luckily, I didn't have to for the rest of the night.

Later that night we were treated to an aerial show like no other. "Puff the Magic Dragon." a converted AC-47, dropped illumination flares and then strafed large sections in front of our lines with its 3, GE mini-guns. They could fire 3 second bursts that would place a 7.62 round every 2 ½ square yards over half the area of a football field. It sounded like a long, continuous (and fearful) dragon's roar.

The official casualty toll for that first night was 26 Marines killed, 50 wounded, but I know there were more walking wounded who hadn't been reported.

September 8, 1967: Lima Company Joins the Fight

The next 2 days, the 8th and the 9th, were relatively quiet compared to all the chaos we had just experienced. At the time, I think that our Command Group wasn't sure if the enemy had simply withdrawn back into hiding or if they were regrouping for another attack. Hindsight now tells us that they were just regrouping.

The weather played a large part in the NVA's decision. The skies were still solidly overcast and this made aerial bombing nearly impossible. Because we were so closely engaged with the enemy, the chances of hitting our own people was too great. We did manage to get some fighter jet runs, but even then, because we were located in an area of hills and valleys, if they didn't come in exactly on a parallel run with our lines, there was a very real danger of hitting our troops. (This very nearly happed to a platoon from Lima Company on September 9th.)

The original Battalion plan was that Lima Company, commanded by Captain Camp, would come down to join us on the Con Thien perimeter after we had completed our initial sweep operation. That's why they weren't with us for the battle on September 7th, but now they were rushing down to join up with us, anxious to join the fight with the rest of their Battalion.

Getting the "Lay of the Land"

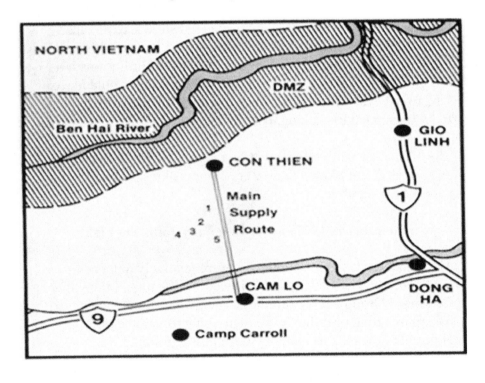

1-   **The Churchyard**

2-   **Bivouac, night of September 8-9**

3-   **Hill 48**

4-   **Hill 88 (Command Post for the 812th NVA Regiment)**

5-   **Small, artillery fire base, C-2**

*   The border between North and South Vietnam was the Ben Hai River.

*   Just a few miles north, both above and below the Ben Hai river, it was suspected that there were several Divisions of NVA (notably, the 324th NVA Division).

*   Con Thien was only a few Kilometers from the border.

*   The MSR (main supply route) was the only way in or out

Over 100 Brave Volunteers Step Up

[*This is a quote from Colonel R.D. Camp's book, "Lima-6, A Marine Company Commander in Vietnam." page 108*]

Colonel Camp: "It was standard procedure to put about 20 men on each truck, so my company of 130-140 Marines needed 7 trucks. When I went out to take charge of the company that morning ... there must have been 270 Marines standing on the roadway, geared up and ready to go."

"It was the biggest formation of Marines I had ever taken over. The majority of the extras were volunteers, many of whom had turned up on their own, without any appeal from me or my sergeants.[74] Others may have reported from standby status. A tremendous feeling of pride came over me to see all these men. When the word went out that the Battalion was in a fight for its life, they grabbed their rifles and gear and joined the convoy getting ready to come to the Battalion's aide.

---

[74] The volunteers were Marines who had been serving in support positions, such as supply clerks, transportation maintenance and drivers, or company clerks. They were not assigned to combat roles, but they were about to join us in one of the largest land battles so far in the war. They knew they would be outnumbered by more than 3-to-1. They knew this, and they still stepped up, and they all served with distinction.

As I stood in front of the formation, I gave the command, 'Right Face!' and 270 men responded with near parade-ground precision. It was very emotional."

It was a great relief to all of us when Lima Company joined us. We had taken a lot of casualties the day before on the 7th, but now, we were almost a full battalion, when you counted all the volunteers that had come with Lima Company.

As the truck transport carrying Lima Company made its way down to us, they passed Cam Lo, then they passed small artillery base, C-2. Finally, as they neared their debarking point to reach us, they saw a large group of Marines walking towards them. It was the detachment we had sent out to guide them to our perimeter positions. There were 4 tanks, along with the detachment, and strapped to each tank were dozens of bodies of the dead and severely wounded from the night before. It must have been a sobering sight, especially for the volunteers because, for most of them, the next few days would be their first and last taste of actual combat.

As the transport trucks were unloading and the casualties were being put on to make the trip back to Dong Ha, they were met with a deadly barrage of enemy rocket and artillery from just across the DMZ. We heard them come over our positions and our first thought was that they were intended for us. The NVA had the entire area we were in mapped out and could hit almost any target with ease. Now, they were expecting reinforcements on the only road into our area. Lima Company took nearly 20 casualties before they were able to off load.

Lt. Dolan Takes Charge of My Platoon

I had made it back to my unit the next morning, and a new Platoon Leader (Lt. Dolan) took over command of our 3rd platoon on September 8th. On the evening of the 8th, we were still on perimeter watch. It was relatively quiet, except for the fact that we had some illumination rounds going off overhead and some artillery landing uncomfortably close. This artillery however was friendly fire, and was coming from Camp Carroll. Our Company Commander (Captain DeBona) got through on the radio and finally got them to stop before we took any friendly fire casualties.

September 9, 1967

We didn't move from our perimeter positions until late on the afternoon of September 9th. Mike Company (my company) was told to take new positions the next day on Hill 48, about 1,000 meters away. Once again, the evening of the 9th passed uneventfully, much the same as the previous one.

September 10, 1967: The Battle for Hill 48

Early that morning of the 10th, our new Battalion Executive Officer, Major Carl Mundy, arrived with a resupply helicopter. This was his first actual experience in a combat situation. Major Mundy would go on to have a long and successful military career, rising to the rank of 3-star General and eventually become the 30th Commandant of the Marine Corps.

What is interesting about this event is that, one, it is unusual for a battalion S-3 (Executive Officer) to be in the field during combat. I suspect that, like many officers, he needed to have combat experience somewhere on his record if he planned to make the military his career. What is also somewhat unusual is that, when looking at all his career assignments that followed, it appears this might have been his only day in the field in a combat situation. He picked a good day for it, he was wounded by shrapnel from NVA artillery and received the Purple Heart.

But the reason I'm mentioning Major Mundy is because, years later, when he was asked to give an account about the Battalion's experiences that day on September 10, he gave an outstanding overview that paints a clear picture of what it was like for the rest of us Marines who were on the perimeter lines. I'm including it here as a preface to the rest of this chapter.

After the rockets hit Hill 48, I ran to the edge of the brush that surrounded the Battalion Command Post. I was struck by the almost theatrical fact that coming across the high ground, to the west of us – and coming across the depression in front of us –was an almost perfect formation of NVA. It looked somewhat like what Andrew Jackson might have encountered in New Orleans as the British came toward him. Here was an almost perfectly aligned NVA Battalion, moving across the low ground toward us, firing their weapons as they came, being supported by mortars and rockets. The Marines in our perimeter were beginning to return fire."

Major Carl Mundy – "Ambush Valley" by Eric Hammel. P. 230

Leading Up to the Battle for Hill 48

The plan for the morning of September 10, 1967 was that the entire Battalion would move from our current location on Hill 48, across the valley, to an adjacent hill.

Early in the morning, our 1st platoon was sent out to do a reconnaissance of the streambed that was running across and just west of our positions on Hill 48. The Battalion still had 2 gunner tanks and a flame tank in operation, and we needed to know if there was a crossing point where we could make it across.

When the 1st platoon returned, they reported that there were no viable crossing points. Additionally, on the other side of the stream bank, they had found an NVA footprint in the wet mud. It was still filling with water so they knew they were very close, possibly just meters away in the dense brush. Having no idea how many there might be, Lt. Crangle reported back via radio and then brought his first platoon back.

The plan was still to move to the adjacent hill, because it was more defensible, but to find a different route. The order of march was, India Company in front and on point, Lima Company on the left flank, Mike Company on the right flank, and Kilo Company in the rear. My Company (Mike Company) was moving out in a wedge formation, which is a highly defensible mobile formation. We had rice paddies 100 meters to the right of us and a hill 100 meters to our left.

3rd Battalion, 26th Marines

September 10, 1967
0730-1430

Key:

⚑ — 3/26 Command Post

←+++++→ — India Company advance to contact

↝↝↝↝↝ — Kilo Company position

◆→◆←◆← — Lima Company advance

▰▰▰ — Lima Company position

⊏▭▭⊐ — Mike Company position
(with platoons as indicated)

This would be the first time Lt. Dolan had commanded our 3rd platoon in the field.
*[From Ambush Valley", page 145]
"When I returned to Mike Company, Captain Andy DeBona told me that John Manzi had been killed. John had been an exceptional platoon commander. His platoon was probably the most aggressive in the company." *Lt. Harry Dolan*
*[From Ambush Valley", page 170]
"The troops never asked questions. I said, "Advance!" and the men advanced. I said, "Stop!" and the men stopped. I said, "Dig in!" and they dug in. They were great troops. They never questioned a single order that I gave them – I owe that to John Manzi who had been a great platoon leader. *Lt. Harry Dolan*
*This was our route of advance until first contact was made by India Company about 1430 hours (2:30 PM) on Sept. 7th .

I could hear over the radio that India Company was reporting that they were taking automatic weapons fire from an unknown size group. Our whole platoon could hear the sound of firing, but when the unmistakable sound of heavy, .51 caliber machine guns could be heard, we knew this was not a squad or small platoon. We knew this was a large unit contact.

Lima Company moved up to support India Company. We had 3 tanks with us and 2 of them were sent to join Lima and India. The 3rd tank was stuck at our point and had broken down. It would later have to be abandoned by the tank crew when they got overrun with NVA soldiers.

We were still on rear guard at this point but knew the shit was about to hit the fan when we heard a new sound, rockets lifting off, a few miles away from across the DMZ. Rockets began landing all around us, targeting our Command Post still on Hill 48, and also, all our companies engaged on the ground. We could see waves of NVA now, out in the rice paddies, leap frogging from dike to dike as they made their way towards us.

Lima Company and India Company, on the adjacent hill, were being pinned down by a single Battalion of NVA. There looked to be another 2 Battalions heading toward us (Mike Company) from across the rice paddies. We were still in our wedge formation, with my platoon was on the left flank, away from the direction of the charge. The NVA started to split their charge in order to try to flank us on our side. We began receiving heavy mortar fire along with more salvos of 140 mm rockets.

My (3rd) platoon took several casualties right away when the initial salvo of rockets came in. Things were really starting to heat up and we were also taking heavy automatic weapons fire as the NVA began trying to break through our lines. I could hear calls for "Corpsman Up!" and I looked around to see where Doc was at. The Lieutenant said he could see Doc O'Connell, going from hole to hole, working on casualties. He was one crazy Scotsman.[75]

Lieutenant Dolan called back to Captain DeBona to give him a status update and the Captain said to "hold the left side of our line." because now our side was experiencing very heavy contact from the front where they were trying to break through. We (the 3rd Platoon) were firing, sometimes blind, at targets hidden in the tall grass, or in the tree line just beyond hand grenade range. On our right, where the 1st Platoon was at, they were coming out of the rice paddies. Then we started to hear the heavy "booms" of artillery coming from across the DMZ, and the incoming high pitched whine of rockets just before they hit and exploded. The NVA to our front were so close

---

[75] I've always believed that the Navy Corpsmen who were assigned to Marine Rifle Companies should just automatically be given citations for bravery.

that even they would hit the ground when they heard the rockets coming in on us.

All you could do was keep your head buried in your helmet and try to get as close to the ground as possible. The hole I had hastily dug needed to be a little wider. In order to get ourselves completely below ground level, the Lieutenant and I needed to really scrunch ourselves in. My left knee, which had started to become infected and was starting to swell from the shrapnel wound the other day, made it so that I couldn't bend it anymore. I was forced to leave my left leg hanging out over the edge. The pant leg was also missing where I had to cut it off. Every now and then, any artillery shell that landed halfway close to our position would drive little tiny pieces of shrapnel into my leg, just above my boot. I was sure that at any time I was going to catch a larger piece that would take my leg completely off.

In those conditions, minutes seemed like hours, and then we would look up and the tree lines were filled with NVA soldiers. When they came out in the open, they would advance in groups of 20 or 30 at a time, firing as they came. As soon as we took one down, more would be coming in his place. There seemed to be a never ending supply of them. I was starting to worry again about running out of ammunition, even though I was now carrying an additional 400 rounds of ammunition. The problem was, I still had only 4 magazines, and that meant I was going to have to use up precious time reloading.

As if things couldn't get any worse, I then heard something that made my blood run cold. It came from the platoon on our right and rapidly passed its way from fighting hole to fighting hole, "Fix Bayonets!" I thought, "Oh shit, here we go again. My old fear of getting bayoneted in the back flashed through my head, and just like 3 nights ago, I slipped a grenade into my left front pocket. It was crazy, but it somehow gave me a feeling of comfort that, if that happened, "Charlie" wasn't going to get away with it.

Things began to ease up just a little bit. What happened was that when the initial NVA charge on Mike Company failed to create a

major breach in our lines and the main body of NVA had turned left
and headed straight up Hill 48, towards our Battalion Command
Post, which Kilo Company was defending. We were still being
assaulted, but now the numbers were more manageable. It was
estimated that a full Battalion of NVA had pinned Lima Company
and India Company near the adjacent hill that was our original
destination, and that we were facing another 2 full battalions, an
additional NVA Heavy Weapons Company, and a Sapper Platoon.
Sappers are the NVA equivalent of Special Forces, trained for
infiltration and demolition.

The decision was made to have Mike Company withdraw back to
help Kilo Company to help protect the Command Post perimeter on
top of Hill 48.

The Company Commander called and said, "Zero Fingers (that was
Lieutenant Dolan's nickname, given to him by the Captain), your 3rd
Platoon will be covering our withdrawal." Lieutenant Dolan
informed him that we didn't have too many effectives left (Marines
still able to fight), but Dolan also knew the rest of the company was
as at least as bad off as we were, so he had us spread out a bit more
and we just waited.

When Captain DeBona began withdrawing our 1st and 2nd Platoons
back to the new perimeter lines, Lt. Dolan started evacuating the
seriously wounded from our Platoon and they went back as well. The
problem was that it would take 1, sometimes 2 Marines to carry a
casualty back, and this was seriously depleting our available
firepower to hold on to our current position.

["A stream of dead and wounded started coming through the company CP
position from Mike-2 and Mike-3 (platoons). ... Captain Andy DeBona, "Ambush
Valley" page 242]

["When I got word to pull back, I started moving WIA's and KIA's back down the
tank trail to the Battalion Command Post. My radio operator (that was me)
collected up some of the M-16s, ammo, and frag grenades from the abandoned
position and started withdrawing. I realized that, in the process of getting our
WIA's and KIA's out, I again had done something stupid – but necessary. The

whole Platoon cover force was now down to two men: myself and my radio
operator." ... Lt. Harry Dolan, "Ambush Valley." page 242]

I remember feeling a dreadful sense of "déjà vu." A similar situation
happened several days ago, when Lt. Manzi and I had made the same
mistake. But now, Lieutenant Dolan and I had another problem. In
all the confusion, now that we were there by ourselves, we weren't
quite sure where we were at, and how to get to the newly established
perimeter.

["My radio operator and I began moving in a low squat along each side of the
tank trail. I could see green .51 caliber tracers lacing the sky overhead. It was a
long 10 to 15 minutes. We heard movement all around us and fired at what we
were sure, by location, must have been the enemy. All of a sudden, coming down
the trail to look for us, standing upright, like he was out for a spring walk, I saw
Captain Andy DeBona. He had come out to find us. I told him to get down because
of the .51 caliber fire. He replied, "Oh bullshit, Zero Fingers, come on. We don't
have all day." .... Lieutenant Harry Dolan, "Ambush Valley." page 242]

Kilo Company, who was defending the Battalion Command Post,
had taken a huge hit just since the time that Mike Company had
begun to withdrawn back to the Battalion perimeter. Now that our 3rd
Platoon was safely evacuated, and Lieutenant Dolan and I had made
it back safely, our 3rd Platoon was once again back inside the
Battalion perimeter. The NVA artillery and rocket salvos were now
concentrating on just two targets The adjacent hill where India and
Lima companies were, and Hill 48, where we were defending the
Battalion Command Post.

The perimeter lines around Hill 48 were in a shambles. The enemy
had made some temporarily breaches across the perimeter lines, but
in almost all instances, they were quickly neutralized.

Our Last Night on Hill 48

Shortly after Lieutenant Dolan and I had gotten back, I lost track of
him and I didn't see him again. At least, that is the last time I
remember seeing him. The remains of our 3rd Platoon had been
placed in different spots to help fill in the many gaps that now
existed in our new defensive perimeter. We had successfully beaten

back several all-out assaults and now the enemy pulled back slightly to the tree lines and other cover. We were finally starting to get more and more air support and bombs and napalm were being dropped on suspected positions. The enemy hadn't completely withdrawn, they were still sending out probing units, testing all around our lines, and that would last for the rest of the evening.

A sergeant came over, grabbed me and another Marine, and walked us to a very large gap in the perimeter line and told us to "pick a fox hole" from any of the 3 empty holes on either side of us. I was shocked to see that many empty fighting holes. I told him I was still looking for the 3rd Platoon, but he said, "Until they tell me differently, this is your platoon now." and he pointed at the empty holes. It was starting to get dark and he showed up twice more, with more Marines, and planted 2 each on either side of us. It was starting to look better, but we were still spread out awfully thin.

The battle was winding down as we began to get increased air support throughout the night. Bombs and illumination flares raked the field in front of us. Puff the Magic Dragon made another pass, but I think it was more for intimidation purposes than anything else. Still, it was an awe-inspiring sight when Puff opened up with her mighty roar.

The enemy would completely disengage by 3 A.M. the next morning of September 11.

My Last Memories of Vietnam

I can remember at one point, having to answer a call of nature. I crawled out of the fighting hole I was in and made my way back behind a large bush (as much for protection from sniper fire as it was for privacy) I was wounded for the 3rd time when I took several pieces of shrapnel, one in my lower right arm and another in the shoulder. I have no idea if it was from an incoming mortar, or if it was friendly fire from one of the bombs dropped too close to our lines, but as I would later find out, it was my ticket home.

I do remember the morning of the next day, on September 11th. I was back with the 3rd Platoon. By now, the most severely wounded had been medevacked out. This was still a very dangerous place to be. Too dangerous to send in helicopters or truck transport to get us out. The road we had come in on was still zeroed in by NVA artillery. We were going to have to walk back to C-2, the small artillery position that we had passed on our way here. A lot of us who were walking wounded were sitting on the ground, waiting for the order to 'saddle up'. Doc O'Connell was helping as many as he could. He stopped and looked at the bandages on my leg. It was still very stiff from the swelling, but someone had evidently given me something for the pain, because I was able to bend my knee more now and I was able to walk with less pain.

I looked at Doc and I saw that he had a large, bloodied bandage around his head. He seemed almost non-responsive when I tried to talk to him. I started yelling for another Corpsman to help him, but he was the only one there. He got up and, in what seemed to be a daze, slowly went over to the next wounded man. After 4 days of holding in all the anxiety, fear, and terror that we all had been through, I almost broke down. It fairly broke my heart to see Doc that way.

I also remember after that, all the bodies of the dead were laid out, prior to being picked up. We were asked to walk through and see if we could positively identify any of the KIA's. They would of course be able to eventually do positive ID's from dog tags or dental records, but this helped hurry up the process. The very first person I looked at, I knew him. It was Edgar Thompson. He had been one of the replacements who was part of my fire team back in early spring. His left arm was missing. I stopped looking at faces after that. I had a part of my brain where I had been sticking images like this … and my brain was beginning to run out of room. The Marines Corps was going to have to identify the rest of those bodies without my help. I walked away.

I remember parts of the 11 kilometer march back from Hill48 to C-2. It was just too dangerous to try to land enough transport helicopters or drive a truck convoy down that road to pick us up. So we got in company formation and walked out. Many of us felt it was the most difficult march we'd ever had to endure while in the Marine Corps.

I remember when we started to approach C-2. We could see the perimeter wire and the center gate we would have to march through. Everyone in Mike Company was completely exhausted at this point, both mentally and physically. Finally, with our destination in sight, we started dragging even more.

Inside the wire was a fairly large group that had come down to meet us. It was composed mostly of a Marine security detail, there to provide escort for the dozen or so news reporters who had been, up until now, following the battle from places like Phu Bai and Danang. This morning, they had been flown down to C-2 to see us when we came in.

Just before we came of the final rise, the Captain must have realized that everyone would be able to see us march in. We looked terrible! Exhausted, dirty, uniforms torn and bloodied, our eyes downcast as we looked at the road underneath our feet, just counting the steps until we were finally able to rest.

We looked like we had been defeated and our Company Commander, Capt. DeBona, sensed that. Just before we got to the top of the rise, he called our column to a halt and we rested for a few moments. Then he said, "We are not going through those gates looking like this! We came into this battle looking like Marines … we kicked ass… and we are going to leave this battle looking like Marines!"

Just then, a loud voice, probably the Company Gunnery Sergeant called the Company to attention. You could hear a collective groan go up (I was part of that). The Gunny gave the order to "Come to Attention! Forward March." and we started marching. "Left, Right, Left." and then he started calling out cadence. Not those fancy marching songs we had gotten used to back in our Pendleton

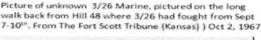

Picture of unknown 3/26 Marine, pictured on the long walk back from Hill 48 where 3/26 had fought from Sept 7-10th. From The Fort Scott Tribune (Kansas)) Oct 2, 1967

YOKE OF WAR rests heavily on the shoulders of this young member of the 3rd Battalion, 26th Marine Regiment, as he uses his M-16 rifle to distribute the weight of his equipment. His group had just completed three days of hard fighting south of Con Thien, Vietnam, where they were continually harassed by enemy artillery rocket barrages.

training, but the standard Marine Corps, boot camp cadence, like a drill instructor would call.

Soon, we were all in synch with the calls, and I could feel my back straightening up, and the limp in my left leg was barely noticeable. I could feel the pounding rhythm through my feet as everyone's boots were hitting the ground at exactly the same time. I looked to my front and to my right and everyone's head was now erect, eyes forward as we marched through the gate.

The crowd from inside of the gate began to spread out on both sides to let us march through. The order came to halt. You could hear and feel all the boots clicking and halting at the same time. After what seemed like many minutes, although it was probably only a few seconds, the order came for "Stand at Ease." and the finally, "Fall Out." We were completely exhausted, but by God, we sure looked like Marines when we were marching in.

We were swarmed by reporters. The NCO's and squad leaders did their best to shoo them away, and they finally started circling around some of the officers to get their stories.

I don't remember anything after that. I don't remember getting picked up, going to Dong Ha, having the shrapnel removed from my leg, arm, and shoulder. Nothing. But I will always remember when we marched back through those gates. It's one of the proudest moments of my entire time in the Marines Corp.

An under strength Battalion of Marines had met the entire 812th NVA Regiment and sent them back behind the DMZ decimated, and it would be several months before they could rebuild enough to be combat ready again. We were broken and bloodied as well, but we had denied them what they were hoping for, and that was to encircle and overwhelm an understrength Battalion of Marines, out in the open field. All they would receive for their troubles was a tremendous ass kicking from us.

I remember parts of being in Okinawa, for about a month, at one of the medical facilities on the base. I remember seeing Sgt. Rhett Holley, who was also getting medical treatment. It was the last time I would see him, or anyone from the old unit for another 47 years.

Duty in Hawaii

I spent the last year and a half in the Marines Corps at a desk job. Originally the Marines Corps tried to put me in an administrative position with the motor pool, but when they discovered that the only pieces on a motor vehicle I recognized were the tires and the steering wheel, they gave up trying to place me and I ended up being assigned to the Marine Corps Post Office at Camp Smith in Hawaii.

While I was in Hawaii, I didn't get off base much. I was still only 19 years old, and the legal drinking age was 20. That meant that when all the other guys would go into town, hitting the bars, I was stuck walking the sidewalks, looking in store windows or walking down by the beach. I eventually was able to sign up for night classes at the University of Hawaii, where I took two classes. One was on "Western Civilization" and the other was an "Introduction to Philosophy." and I really enjoyed both classes. After my evening classes were over I would sometimes go over to the East-West Center where there was a beautiful amphitheater. I would get a cup of coffee and sit out on a veranda where they had a large garden area with a stream running through it. You could hear all kinds of exotic night sounds and I remember someone telling me that they had even gone to the trouble of importing bull frogs from the Mississippi River. I don't know if that was true or not, but you could hear them bellowing in the quiet evenings.

I particularly remember the sounds of crickets in the quiet darkness. Sometimes they would be so loud it would almost drown out the bull frogs. I wrote about that to my Mom in one of my letters. I only mention that because I came to find out that they didn't actually have crickets there, it was a result of the tinnitus I had developed in Vietnam. I still have it to this day, it's constant, and it's every bit as loud as when I first acquired it. There's no cure for tinnitus, and some people have a real problem with that, but for me, it's forever tied to my memories of the quiet times I spent in Hawaii, in the evenings, at the East-West Amphitheater, listening to the bull frogs and the crickets. Sometimes it even helps put me to sleep.

I was well enough now to go back to regular duty, but my official record was stamped with the notation that said I could not go back into a combat zone until September of 1969, which was 3 months after my enlistment would be up. If I had wanted to go back to Vietnam, or wanted to go on to OCS (Officers Candidate School), I would have to wait a year and a half, then re-enlist for another 4-6 years. I did have one other option, I could petition for a waiver, to be sent back to a combat zone but I had no interest in that at all. Everyone I knew from 3/26 had been either rotated back to the states, or had been medically evacuated like me, or, they were dead.

From Hawaii, I was transferred back to Camp Pendleton, where I spent the last year of my enlistment. When I first arrived at my new "desk job" job assignment at the 5th Marine Division's Central Post Office, I was determined to make one more serious attempt to get transferred back to what I considered "the real Marine Corps." When I first reported to my new Commanding Officer, I was going to request to be sent to NCO school. I figured that if I couldn't get into Officer's Training School without signing reenlistment papers, at least I would try to make some additional enlisted rank during my last year.

Reporting for Duty at Camp Pendleton

Back in Hawaii, all the enlisted men wore green fatigue uniforms when they worked at the post office, so that's what I was wearing when I marched into the administrative offices. I got directions to the Colonel's office and was told I would first need to report in to the Gunnery Sergeant, whose office was next door to the Colonels. I opened his door, marched up to his desk and with my orders in hand and said, "Good morning Gunnery Sergeant. Lance Corporal Ward, reporting for duty. I was told to see you before reporting to the Colonel."

The "Gunny" gave me a long, cold stare. He looked like one of those old time Marines with a short, buzz haircut, wiry build, and a flamboyant, handlebar mustache that gave him quite an intimidating look. The Gunny just continued to stare at me, like I was some complete idiot who had just popped up out of the thin air, with the express intention of ruining his otherwise perfect day.

I won't bore you with his long tirade, but the gist of it was that I was an embarrassment to the uniform, an embarrassment to the Marines Corps, and to him in particular. He went on to say that he couldn't understand how I could have the gall to show up for duty, wearing green and expect to be allowed into the Colonel's office. He wrapped it all up by saying that I had exactly 15 minutes to get back to my barracks, change into a Class A uniform, and be back there standing tall in front of his desk. And then he added that I shouldn't be expecting to be there for very long, because he was going to personally have me shipped over to Vietnam ... because the only thing "my sorry ass" was good for was "cannon fodder." And with that, I turned and fairly ran (hobbled) out of the office and all the way back to my barracks. For some crazy reason, I believed every word he had said to me.

Luckily, my Class A uniform was hung and pressed and sitting in my locker. Then I pulled out my dress shoes and gave them a quick, high gloss shine by spraying them with Pledge and buffing them as soon as they dried (an old trick that works fairly well for the first hour or so, then the shine starts to scuff up rather quickly … but it would be long enough for me to get past the Gunny's inspection).

When I finally got back to the Gunny's office, the door was closed. I took a moment to catch my breath and then knocked on the door, opened it up and stepped inside. The Gunny was standing up by his filing cabinet, looking at some papers, and as soon as he saw it was me, without any change in facial expression, he said, "Oh, hey Ward, good timing, the Colonel's got a few minutes." And with that he opened the door to the Colonel's office and we both walked in. I WAS VERY, VERY CONFUSED. I followed behind him and marched directly towards the Colonel's desk, stopped in front of it, came to attention, and said, "Lance Corporal Ward, reporting for duty … Sir!

The Gunny still had my personnel file, and the copies of my orders, and he handed both to the Colonel. The Colonel told me to "Stand at ease." as he proceeded to look at my papers. It was then that I noticed the Gunnery Sergeant's uniform. I could tell by the hash marks on his sleeve that he'd been in the Marine Corps for at least 3 enlistments. And then I looked at the ribbons on his uniform and I recognized that he had never served in Vietnam, or the Korean conflict for that matter, and that he only had a half dozen ribbons. On the other hand, I (the 19-year old, sorry ass recruit) had twice that many, and most of them for being in combat. It's then that I realized he must have mistaken me for a newbie when I first arrived. That explained a lot, and I came to find out later that that was how the Gunny treated all the new, incoming young Marines. It was just a little ritual of his. (*The Gunny turned out to be a really good character, and everyone, including myself, would look forward to the little tirades that he would pull on new recruits.*)

The Colonel dismissed the Gunny, and then had me sit down in one of the big chairs in front of his desk. We talked for a few minutes, and then I asked for permission to "speak freely." I told him about my desire to go to NCO School, and that I'd really like to get back into the infantry field, but he was very honest with me and said that was highly unlikely, unless of course I was willing to commit to signing back up for another enlistment. Then he said that he'd noticed that I had had previous experience in the post office, both in Hawaii, and for a short time before I enlisted. He said that he would rather have me work at the main post office there for a few weeks, just to get acclimated, and then he wanted to put me at one of the small post office branches that they had at Camp San Mateo. He wanted me to be the "temporary postmaster." It's normally a position that is held by an officer, but he had an opening that wasn't going to be filled for several months. I thanked the Colonel and told him I would be glad for the opportunity. I eventually transferred to Camp San Mateo and held that position, along with 3 other PFC's, who would work for me for the next 6 months. They were a good bunch, and it was a quiet place. I enjoyed my time at Camp San Mateo very much.

When I was finally replaced by a new officer at Camp San Mateo, I went back to the main office at Camp Pendleton and finished out the rest of my enlistment. By now, I had lost all interest in making a career out of the service, even though, towards the end, the reenlistment officer did offer a modest bonus and also offered to send me to Officer's Training School. But, it was too late, my mind was made up.

On May 29, 1969, I received an honorable discharge from the Marine Corps and boarded a plane for home. I was happy to get back to Iowa, but it was also with a certain amount of mixed feelings. I felt like I had left something unfinished. I didn't get a job right away, and instead spent most of the summer getting ready for college in the fall.

COMING HOME

Chapter 10

Coming Home

When I finally got back to Colfax, I was both relieved, and a bit surprised that my return seemed to go unnoticed by most people, and that included my own family. No one really talked about the war. I had noticed the same thing when I started school at UNI[76] in Cedar Falls. I'm sure that, like all college campuses, there were ongoing demonstrations about the war, but they never rose to the level of attention where I became aware of them. But, I wasn't complaining, I would probably not have been comfortable talking about it.

The Parade

It was spring of the following year, and I was back in Colfax. The commute to Cedar Falls was only 2 ½ hours, and I rarely spent weekends there. The Memorial Day celebrations were coming up, and I got a call from Royal Cross who was in charge of the American Legion's[77] Color Guard that marched in the parade every year. Royal explained that this year they wanted to have, besides the regular Legion Color Guard, a representative of one member from each branch of the service. These four veterans would march in the parade along with the American Legion Color Guard. Royal was concerned about whether or not I still had my old uniform.

I wasn't very keen on the idea at first, but it turned out that they already had commitments from some of my old school buddies, who would be representing the Army, the Air Force, and the Navy. I was the only one available to represent the Marines Corps, so I finally agreed.

My biggest worry was whether I would still fit in the old uniform.

---

[76] University of Northern Iowa.

[77] American Legion in Colfax, Iowa. See Chapter 10, Chapter Notes at the back of the book.

Two semesters of college life can put a strain on even the fittest of figures. Happily, I still fit. I'd put on about 10 pounds, but it hadn't gone to my waistline yet. I had my Class-A uniform pressed, and I took special care to put a high shine on my dress shoes and polished the brass on my belt buckle. When the morning of the parade came around, I was ready to go.

Our instructions had been to meet first at the Colfax American Legion Hall, where Royal would give us a quick rundown on the schedule of activities and what the order of march was going to be. I drove down that morning, parked in the lot, and saw that there were a number of people gathering in the ground floor dining hall area. As I walked in, I spotted a small group in the corner. They were the other veterans that had been asked to represent the various branches of the service. I walked over and said, "hello." They'd been talking among themselves, but looked up as I approached. There was a short acknowledgement as they stared at me, and then they turned back and continued their conversation.

Feeling a little awkward, I looked around the room, and spotted Royal, talking to several members of his Color Guard. After all these years, I can't remember the names of some of the older members except for Harold Taylor[78]. They were all wearing their American Legion dress uniforms, which were a dark blue or black, with white service belts, boots, and helmets, all except for Colonel Cross of course, who was Commander of the Guard. He wore a gold helmet. They were what we would call today, members of the "old guard." They were all very impressive looking, and to this day, whenever I think of a Veteran's Day parade, I am reminded of them.

When I checked in with Royal, he asked me to stand by for a few minutes and then he'd get us all together and go over the schedule. So, there I was, sitting on a chair next to one of the empty tables, just waiting for things to get started. After a few minutes, I looked down at my watch, and just happened to glance up in time to see the first

---

[78] I have since learned that Ed Jones and Harry Rosenbaum were also members of the Legion Color Guard at that time.

group I had met when I came it. There were standing by the front door. Evidently they had called Royal over to discuss something with him. The conversation had started to become a bit more animated. Then, just as suddenly, it stopped, and everyone's attention was directed towards me. I started to wonder if I had done something wrong.

Reluctantly, it seemed, Royal began walking over in my direction. I was a little more than curious to see what this was all about. Royal stood directly in front of me, and I straightened up as if at attention. I noticed that he was staring at the ribbon decorations that I was wearing on my uniform. It seemed as if he was counting them, or deciphering what each one was for. After what seemed like a very long time, and without saying anything to me, he turned and left.

I looked over again at the original group, the ones who had initiated the conversation in the first place, and it started to slowly sink into my brain what this was all about. The group of younger veterans had felt there was a problem. It seems that they believed I was wearing decorations on my uniform that I wasn't entitled to[79]&[80], and they had voiced their concern about that. It was a serious accusation and no small matter. Later, I even heard that there had been a  suggestion that *I should not be allowed to be in the parade at all*, walking alongside other veterans.

---

[79] In hindsight, I have found out that the top 3 decorations look very different on a Marine's uniform, as opposed to an Army uniform, even though they are for the exact same things. This may have contributed to the confusion.

[80] Purple Heart, with 2 gold stars, representing 2 additional presentations of the medal, the Combat Action Ribbon (highly prized in all branches of the military), the Presidential Unit Citation, Vietnam Gallantry Cross with Oak Leaf, Vietnam Civil Action Ribbon with/Oak Leaf, Vietnam Service Ribbon, Vietnam Campaign Ribbon, National Defense Medal, Good Conduct Medal, and Marine Rifle Sharpshooter Award.

It is difficult to describe all the feelings that I was experiencing at that moment. A great part of it was anger. A disproportionate amount of anger, so much so that it even startled me. At the same time, I also felt a great deal of embarrassment, and I don't know why, but I also felt shame. Shame because, right at that moment, it seemed to me that everyone in the room was staring at me and I had to wonder what they must be thinking. Were they thinking that "I was dishonoring myself, my uniform, and all the other veterans who had assembled here for the parade?"

I felt a great helplessness. There was no way I could prove any differently, not right then, not unless I drove all the way back home, dug through all my records, and returned with my discharge and awards papers. The anger, embarrassment, and the shame were all mixing together. I felt like I was going to explode.

And then something happened. It seemed like such a small thing at the time, but it was enough to take the lid off the pending explosion. Royal, who I think was feeling just about as bad about the whole thing as I was, had been talking to Harold Taylor, and Royal had evidently asked Harold to come over and take a look.

When Mr. Taylor got in front of me, just like Royal had, he took a long look at the ribbons, and then looked up, directly into my eyes … and he nodded. Just that simple, he nodded, as if in recognition that everything was OK. And then he turned back in Royal's direction and nodded, and without a word, he went back to the group he was with. And that, as they say, was that. The "old guard", the WWII veterans had accepted me, even if some of the younger veterans had not.

It took me a while to cool down, but I realized that there was nothing I could do except finish what I'd started. The parade was about to begin. I took my place with the others, and we marched up Main Street, up to the cemetery where the ceremonies were taking place, and after that, back down Main Street. When we had finally gotten to the end of the parade route, I walked to my car and I drove home. Once I was home, I took off my uniform, left the ribbons on my shirt. I put it all in a box and never looked at them again. Over time, the box was lost, and I'd never thought about them again.

I spent the better part of that day sitting out in my back yard, drinking too many beers, and trying to sort through everything that had happened. I came to the conclusion that there was no way I was going to reconcile with it, and still have any dignity left. I decided to do what I had done before, just put everything away -- the anger, the hurt, the shame I was feeling, into that little locked box in my mind where I kept all the other feelings I'd felt from Vietnam. I thought that I made the right decision, but when I look back at it now, after all these years, I only have two regrets. For one, I should have stayed around after the parade and confronted my friends about it. I should have just walked right over there and dealt with it at the time, but I didn't. I was only 20 years old. What did I know about anything?

The other regret I have was that I never went back and told Mr. Taylor how much his gesture had meant to me. If I had, I would have found out that he himself had been a Marine during WWII, and that would have explained so much, and why he instinctively trusted me. He and I were both Marines, and had been taught the same credo (which is still taught to all Marines today.),

Harold Taylor **USMC** 1943
courtesy of Beverly Taylor

"There are only two things to always remember: You never lie, and you never quit. Everything else is pretty much open to interpretation." Semper Fi, Harold Taylor

Getting On with My Life

I spent the next 28 years working for Cummins Diesel in Des Moines, Iowa. It was a job I grew to enjoy, especially in the last 10 years, during the 90's, when I was given a job in Advanced Information Products. From there, I went to work for a big electronics company in Boise, Idaho. Finally, my wife and I relocated here in Florida, and I went to work for a startup venture company as a software systems developer. Throughout all that time, I never got involved with any veteran's activities or organizations.

About 6 years ago, my health finally became enough of an issue that I wasn't able to maintain a full-time job. I took early retirement at age 62 and tried to develop a private consulting business that I could do from home. Unfortunately, my particular field was automotive networks and vehicle telematics. I received several short-term projects, but they all were coming from off-shore companies that would eventually require that I travel. I was also discovering that the very things that I had loved about the work I was doing, the excitement of challenges, taking on new projects, and working against deadlines, was causing more problems with my heart. It finally came to a head in January of 2010, when I was interviewing for a position as project manager on a large, county-wide municipal bus application. I had a "heart event" during the interview. I'd been without any health insurance for a least 6 months and I knew I was going to have to go to the VA.

The VA Experience

I actually dreaded the thought of going there. It seemed impossible to me that, after all these years, I would even be eligible for benefits. By then I had spent nearly 45 years avoiding any thoughts about my past experiences, and I barely even knew why I felt the way that I did. But, the anxiety was very real.

The first time I tried to take the twenty-minute drive up to the hospital, I ended up overshooting the exit and winding up in Port St. Lucie, twenty miles north of there. I drove back home, mentally and physically exhausted, and I vowed to go again the next morning. The next day I made it all the way up to the hospital's parking lot, where I would need to grab a bus shuttle to the main buildings. I sat on the bench in the parking lot and let several buses pass by before I finally got on one. Without belaboring the point any longer, by the end of that day, I realized how I had been wrong to have put this off for so long. (I describe my experiences with the VA in the concluding section of this book.)

Reconnecting with Old Comrades

Shortly after I had enrolled in the VA Medical program, I received a call. The voice was immediately familiar; it was Rhett Holley, my old squad leader. It had been nearly 46 years since I last saw him, when we parted ways after our hospital stay in Okinawa.

We must have talked for nearly two hours on the phone as he told me about old comrades who were still around, and who had passed. From the old squad, nearly half were gone. But what surprised me the most was how many of them had been afflicted with many of the same medical issues that I had, and like me, those issues had manifested themselves much earlier than in the general population. The effects of our exposure to Agent Orange were taking their toll.

Rhett and I stayed in regular contact from that day forward. During a visit we had last year, he talked about one of the goals he had set for himself, which was to write a book about his personal experiences in Vietnam. He wanted to leave something for his family and his grandchildren, to whom he rarely had spoken about those times. I was honored to be able to help him with some of the editorial tasks that were involved, and although Rhett was not a natural writer, I and several of his closest friends kept reminding him to just write with his own voice, and don't worry about the punctuation, we'd take care of that. When his book was finally published, I could only sit back and admire the outstanding job he had done. [81]

Making Peace with the Past

Although I received outstanding service from the VA hospital, the VA Claims Division turned out to be a real nightmare. I had filed a disability claim because my heart issues (IHD[82]) were directly attributable to Agent Orange Exposure. The initial claim was

---

[81] "Memories of an Old Marine" – Calvin Rhett Holley.

[82] Ischemic Heart Disease and Arterial Stenosis. I am currently rated at 100%, Service Connected, Permanent & Total Disability.

rejected due, more or less, to a clerical error on the first page of the form. Normally that would not be a problem, and so I submitted a new form. What I did not know was that once a claim is rejected, it is put into another pile, and then basically ignored. In my case, it would take another three and a half years before they even looked at it again.

My Experiences with the Disability Claim Process

On my first visit to the hospital, besides healthcare, I was also scheduled to see a VSO (Veteran's Service Officer). The VSO's job is to help the veteran determine if he or she has any service connected issues, and if so, to help them file a claim with the VA Regional Office in St. Petersburg.

I did end up filing a claim for damage to my left knee from shrapnel wounds. I'd had three operations on it after leaving the service, and as a result, I have arthritis in the knee and hip. But, most importantly, I'd been diagnosed with ischemic heart disease. The VA was still not recognizing ischemic heart disease as a result of Agent Orange exposure at that time, but the VSO insisted that I file a claim for IHD, as well.

My claim was filed in January of 2010. The next step was to have a VA doctor's examination scheduled. I knew that, in general, claims were running way behind, and I expected to have to wait for several months. I waited, and waited. Nine months later, after a number of phone inquiries, I received a letter from the VA denying my claim for injury to the left knee and disallowing my claim for exposure to Agent Orange[83]. The claims were being rejected outright. The claims examiner stated in his letter that, after thoroughly reviewing my records, "*He had determined that, although I had been assigned duty in Vietnam, my MOS (military occupation specialty) was that of a "clerk" and not as a combat infantryman, as I had stated.*" The

---

[83] At the time, the VA was not recognizing Ischemic Heart Disease as being associated with AO exposure. It would be another year before they would.

denial letter went on to say, "*And we opine that, although you may have been exposed to loud noises, it is unlikely that you would be exposed to mortar fire as you said.*"

I can still remember the day, and the circumstances, that took place when I read that letter. I'd driven down to the mail drop box to pick up our mail. When I saw that there was letter from the claims division, I opened it immediately to read what it said. The shock of reading the claim adjuster's reasons for denial was like getting hit in the chest with a hammer.

Disbelief turned to anger, which turned to extreme angina pain. The angina was so bad that I dropped to the ground and laid there for nearly 10 minutes before I dared to try to get back and into my car. The shock of the experience shook me up so badly that, for a while, I completely forgot about the letter, and all I could think about was whether or not I needed to call for an ambulance.

The worst part of it all was that I found out there was really nothing to be done about the denial letter, other than to file an appeal. There are no phone numbers to call, no addresses to write to, that will give you any other answer. There is only the appeals process, and that too often does take years. In my case, it took another 3 years.

"Top Sheeting" – A Tool in the Claims Denial Toolbox

Over the course of the next few months, I talked to a lot of people in veterans' assistance organizations, both at the state level and the national level. I also talked to a number of people on veterans' support lines who were familiar with what was happening. I was only one of many veterans who had been denied by an unofficial process, used by claims adjusters, and known to unlucky veterans as "Top Sheeting." What happens is this, a claim adjuster is swamped with new claims and now there was a new directive from the VA to "clear these new claims within 125 days." The adjusters began to develop certain questionable strategies to accommodate the new directive to "clear new claims." As a means of being able to achieve their goal of clearing new claims, the claims adjusters would develop shortcuts. One popular shortcut was to look at the very top sheet (the veteran's discharge paper, DD-214) and if anything, even a typo, was present that would sidetrack the claim, the claim was promptly denied and effectively taken off their desk and forwarded somewhere else. At the same time (for the claims examiner), it still counted as a "new claim" being processed, and it even counted towards potential bonus money for them, because they had "processed the new claim within the timeframe of the new directive."

My claim was eventually sent to a huge stack of files labeled, "Under Appeal." This was now a totally different category, and the VA was not taking heat for this particular category yet, only the "New Claims" category.

What had happened was this: my original claim consisted of my discharge paper (a single sheet on top) and all the subsequent documents in my service file that pertained to my combat records and how, where, and when I had received my wounds. The claims adjuster read the very first paragraph, on the top sheet of my discharge papers, and saw that I had finished up my time in the Marine Corps at a desk job working as a postal clerk. For that particular examiner, this was just what he had been looking for and everything came to a screeching halt, and he stamped my claim "Denied." He even wrote a nasty little note along with the denial letter intimating that he didn't believe I had ever been in combat). My claim was now officially, "Denied."

It would take 3 more years before the VA Claims Division would even look at my case again. In that time, friends made sure I didn't give up, comrades from my old unit even wrote personal letters.

During that time, I was getting very frustrated and wanted to just drop it, but Rhett Holley (my old squad leader) talked to a good friend and high school classmate of his, Estus Whitfield[84]. Estus (an ex-Navy Captain) called me up immediately, and said, "You don't know me, so let me tell you the way it's going to be. You don't give up until I do. And I never give up!" When I finally got off the call, I was starting to feel sympathy for any poor SOB's that stood in this man's way.

In the end, the claim appeal was reopened, and I was finally able to get a new evaluation scheduled. This time, I requested that instead of using the Claims Division's medical specialist, I wanted to have a regular staff physician from the VA hospital perform the evaluation. I got some push back on that request, with the admonition that, "if I failed to make the appointment at the prescribed time, they would possibly drop my claim altogether." This didn't put me off in the least, I left for my appointment two hours early, just in case I had car trouble.

I spent the first part of the morning sitting in the cafeteria, drinking coffee, and worrying about what the exam would be like this time. My first exam, three years ago, had been a complete disaster. I reminded myself that this time, I wasn't going to fall into the trap of answering just "Yes or No" to the questions they would ask, even if that annoyed them.

I was ushered into an empty office and told to have a seat while the doctor was finishing up with his last session. After just a few minutes, the doctor walked in and I felt an immediate rush of relief when I saw that it wasn't the lady doctor from three years ago. This doctor was tall, middle-aged, and although he had an intimidating appearance, his demeanor seemed friendly.

As he sat down at his desk, he picked up some paper work, which I assumed had the questions he was supposed to ask me, but he pause

---

[84] Estus Whitfield was one of Rhett Holley's friends and classmates from high school. Estus is retired military, a Naval Captain (that is 1 step down from a Rear Admiral). He is also a long time environmental consultant (to 4 "sitting" Florida governors) and a lifelong environmental activist.

and then said, "Now, just to make it clear, I'm only here to evaluate the results of your most recent stress test, and ask a few questions. The final decision on your disability claim will always be determined by the claim adjusters in St. Petersburg." And with that, he started to ask me the same questions that I had gotten before. This time, however, after I would answer each question as a "Yes or No." I was quick to add how I felt after that activity. This didn't seem to agitate him at all, as it had the doctor in my first exam, but, when we finally concluded the interview, he again repeated what he had said earlier, that the results of his evaluation held little sway over the adjusters in St. Petersburg.

I was starting to feel a little sick at this point. I knew this was my last chance for a reevaluation, and it seemed like no matter what my cardiologists at the VA were finding, or my other doctors were saying, the disability evaluation was going to follow a whole different set of rules and was going to be decided by the same guy who accused me of being a postal clerk in Vietnam. It's difficult to describe how I felt right at that moment. The only words I can use to describe it would be to say that I felt abandoned. I felt like I had all those years ago when I had shown up to march in the Memorial Day parade.

I think the doctor must have sensed my disappointment, and he asked, "Do you have any other questions?" I don't know why I said what I did next, but I just looked at him and said, "Yeah, I guess I'm wondering why, if I'm supposed to be in such good shape, why I feel the way I do … every day?"

The doctor just stared at me for the longest time, neither of us saying anything, and then he said, "If you can just bear with me for a while longer, I want to check on some things." and with that he got up out of his chair and left the room. It was over 20 minutes before he came back, and the friendly demeanor seemed to have disappeared. He didn't seem to be angry with me, because when he sat back down at his desk and started typing on his computer, he turned to me and said, "Just give me a few more minutes, I want to write up some personal notes for your report."

To me, this seemed like it could only be a good thing, although I had no idea what he was doing. He'd been typing for a while, and then he turned and said, "Like I mentioned before, the claim adjuster makes the final decisions, but I going to interject some of my opinions on this report." He typed a little more, and then turned to me once again and said, "I don't know what your final claim rating is going to be … but it's going to be a significant increase. And it's going to go all the way back to when you first filed your claim." When he finally finished his typing, he stood up (the exam was now officially over), and he said to me, "Thank you for your service." All I could say in return was, "Doctor, thank you for your service."

 As I was walking away, I was so happy, and I felt so vindicated, that I could start to feel the angina pain swell up in my chest (it works both ways you know), but I didn't care, I just found a place to sit down, took one of my nitro pills, and sat there and enjoyed the moment.

Approximately 3 weeks later, I received word that my disability claim for Ischemic Heart Disease, due to Agent Orange exposure, had been granted, unconditionally, at 100%. My long wait was finally over, and although I was overjoyed about that, I also felt a sadness for all the people I had met along the way who are still battling with that same part of the system.

But, I have to say that the VA in general, especially the medical services; the doctors, nurses, and their aides who work there, have been fantastic, and they have continued to be since the first day I walked in the VA hospital doors.

August 7th – "Purple Heart Day"

Just about 2 years ago, in 2014, something very special happened, that meant a lot to both Rhett Holley and myself. We each received a letter from Senator Maria Sachs, one of our Florida state senators.

She was co-sponsoring a bill to establish August 7th as the official "Purple Heart Day" in Florida.

Senator Sachs found out that Rhett had been born here (in Niceville, Florida) and that I had moved here some years back. She also found out that we had both served in the same unit and we both had been wounded a total of 3 times each. She asked Rhett and I to represent the "faces of Florida Purple Heart veterans" for a news conference she was scheduling. Senate Sachs had Senate Proclamations issued and presented to both of us.

A Senator's Proclamation
by Senator Maria Sachs

A Proclamation recognizing Bill Ward for his honorable service to his country and for his continued advocacy for the recognition of all who served and sacrificed in time of war.

WHEREAS, Bill Ward was born July 1, 1948 in Colfax, Iowa and currently resides in Boynton Beach, where he has lived since 2003, and

WHEREAS, Bill Ward began his military service in July 1966, training at San Diego and Camp Pendleton as a Marine rifleman and serving in combat radio operations in the Mike Company, 3rd Battalion, 26th Marine Regiment, and

WHEREAS, over the course of a 6-month period in 1967, Bill Ward, on three occasions suffered lacerations and shrapnel wounds during firefights, including the 4-day Battle of Hill 48 in Con Thien, Vietnam, during which 350 Marines were killed or wounded, and

WHEREAS, over the course of his service, Bill Ward was awarded three Purple Hearts, the National Defense Medal, the Vietnamese Service Medal with 1-star, the Combat Action Ribbon, the Presidential Unit Citation, the Vietnam Gallantry Cross Medal, the Vietnamese Civil Actions Medal, the Vietnamese Campaign Medal[85] , a Rifle Sharpshooter Award, and a Good Conduct Medal, and

WHEREAS, Bill Ward was honorably discharged from the service on May 1, 1969, having attained the rank of Lance Corporal E-3, and

WHEREAS, Bill Ward is a passionate advocate for all veterans and is tireless in his support for the adoption of legislation in this state

---

[85] In the Senator's Proclamation, they omitted the Vietnamese Campaign Medal and incorrectly duplicated the Combat Action Ribbon in its place. The above text corrects that.

designating August 7 as "Purple Heart Day." a day when public officials, schools, private organizations, and all residents of this state are encouraged to honor those wounded or killed while serving in any branch of the Unites States Armed Services, and

WHEREAS, Bill Ward remains committed to honoring those who did not return home with their fellow warriors, noting the importance of recognizing them, and especially their families and friends who lost a loved one, NOW, THEREFORE,

I, **Senator Maria Lorts Sachs, of Florida Senate District 30**, do hereby recognize Bill Ward for his honorable service to his country and for his continued advocacy for the recognition of all who served and sacrificed during times of War.

....

In 1992, I once again had the privilege of working with the military. I was employed at the time with Cummins Engine Company as a sales and support manager of advanced electronic products for Cummins Diesel Engines in Des Moines, Iowa. One of the Cummins engines is utilized exclusively in the Army's M2 and M3 Bradley Fighting Vehicle[86] and other model Cummins' engines are in dozens of other military transport vehicles.

Purely as an exercise, I applied for Cummins to be awarded a government contract to supply replacement parts to the Camp Dodge, National Maintenance Training Center[87]. I met with their people and discovered that they were in desperate need of training tools and technical training for their instructors, but their current budget wouldn't allow for most of the upgrades they needed. I made

---

[86] The M2 Bradley holds a crew of three (a commander, a gunner and a driver) as well as six fully equipped soldiers. The M3 mainly conducts scout missions and carries two scouts in addition to the regular crew of three, with space for additional TOW missiles.

[87] Camp Dodge had become the primary training facility in the United States for vehicle maintenance technicians.

a call to the Cummins National Headquarters in Columbus, Indiana to see if there was any help that we could give them, and I was absolutely shocked at the immediate and total commitment that was forthcoming. Training tools, training literature valued at nearly $50,000, at no charge. Additionally, Cummins set up annual training sessions for the Camp Dodge instructors, with Cummins' engineers who flew in to give train-the-trainer instruction sessions, and this too was also at no charge. Cummins had recognized that there was a huge amount of equipment returning from the first Gulf War and they were in drastic need of repair, and that Army training budgets were tight, so Cummins committed to step up and fill that void. General Thompson, from the Red River, Texas Military Depot[88] (now the largest U.S. maintenance depot) flew up to attend the ceremonies being held at Camp Dodge to congratulate me.

I was overwhelmed that I would be given credit for all of this. It seemed to me that I had only put the ball on motion, and that many others had shouldered the hard work. But sometimes, you just have to keep your mouth shut, smile, and accept the award. That strategy paid off, because the following year, they did they very same thing, and I won the Governor's Volunteer Award for a 2nd time in 1994 [89].

I continued to work directly with the Camp Dodge Training Facility for the next six years, until I moved on to take a job with Preco Electronics, in Boise, Idaho in 2001.

---

[88] The Red River Depot's maintenance mission includes the repair, rebuild, overhaul and conversion of tactical wheeled vehicles, as well as the Army's light tracked combat vehicle fleet.

[89] I actually put together a number of special programs for the National Guard Training Center that were designed to accommodate their way of doing business, as opposed to ours, and this was another reason that I was chosen to receive the award for a 2nd year in a row. The name of the award is "Governor's Volunteer Award for Civilian Defense" and it is not given every year, only when there is deemed to be an appropriate recipient.

tion in December 1991 from the ... welcome to come in and visit.

6-3-1993
Jasper Cty Tribune

Bill Ward Presented Award

At the annual recognition ceremony held May 7 at Camp Dodge, Bill Ward, Colfax, was presented the Governor's Volunteer Recognition Award for outstanding volunteer service to the State of Iowa by Governor Terry Branstad. The award was presented in recognition of Bill's help in developing a maintenance training program for the Iowa National Guard. The Camp Dodge training facility is now the largest of its kind in the U.S. Its mission is to train military personnel to support both transportation and armored vehicles in the field.

And finally, I would like to recognize the following people who have been inspirational figures in my life.

- 1st Lieutenant John Manzi, KIA, 9/7/67   USMC

- Sergeant Rhett Holley   USMC

- Corporal Bill Halsey   USMC

- Corporal George Eriksson   USMC

- Navy Corpsman Scott O'Connell   USN
  (Corpsman of Marines)

- Captain Estus Whitfield,   (retired)   USN
  who, besides being a close, personal friend, worked tirelessly to both encourage and help Sergeant Holley and myself to write our stories. Without his initial help, our stories may likely never have been written.

The first advice that I received when I got to Vietnam was from Sgt. Rhett Holley, he said ...

"Watch these men [90]. Learn to walk the way they walk, and move the way they move, and maybe, just maybe, you might make it!"

These were men who taught me not to hesitate, but rather, to run towards the sound of gunfire.

---

[90] Sgt. Holley was pointing at Eriksson and Halsey when he said that.

To the men of the **3ʳᵈ battalion, 26ᵗʰ Marine Regiment** that I served
with, this plaque was commissioned to show the casualties they
suffered during their first 10 months in Vietnam, up until the final
battle, in early September of 1967 near Con Thien, at Hill 48, where
we took on, and defeated the 812ᵗʰ NVA Regiment.

**Each row represents 70 casualties (either KIA or
wounded).**

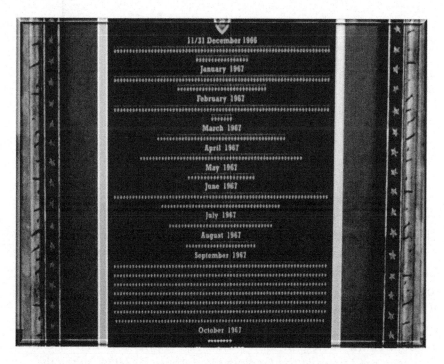

The September, 1967 casualties, near Con Thien, resulted in 489
Marines, either killed or wounded for the entire month. This was
nearly 50% of our Battalion and came to be the deadliest month in
the Battalion's long history. Each Purple Heart icon in the above
picture represents a casualty (either KIA or WIA).

Chapter Notes

Foreword Section Notes:

The DMZ

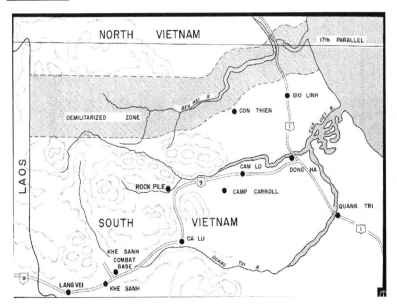

The Demilitarized Zone (DMZ) was a buffer zone between North and South Vietnam. It ran along the Ben Hai River from the South China Sea in the east, to the Vietnam-Laos border on the west at roughly the 17th parallel. This is near the center of present-day Vietnam, and extended roughly 5 kilometers on both sides of the river. The DMZ's width varied from 3- 6 kilometers in most places to about 10 kilometers in some others. The DMZ was a combat-free area as agreed upon at the Geneva Conference in 1954, when the French and Viet Minh came to an agreement to secure peace in Vietnam. For the most part, the U.S. honored this restriction during the Vietnam War.

Kansas City Records Fire

On July 12, 1973, a disastrous fire at the National Personnel Records Center (NPRC) destroyed approximately 16-18 million Official Military Personnel Files (OMPF). The records affected:

Branch	Personnel and Period Affected	Estimated Loss
Army	Personnel discharged November 1, 1912 to January 1, 1960	80%
Air Force	Personnel discharged September 25, 1947 to January 1, 1964 (with names alphabetically after Hubbard, James E.)	75%

No duplicate copies of these records were ever maintained, nor were microfilm copies produced.

Marine Regimental Command Unit Structures

26th **Maine Regiment** Consisted of Three Battalions
    1st Battalion, 2nd Battalion, 3rd **Battalion**

3rd **Battalion** Consisted of Four Rifle Companies, a Headquarters Company, and a Weapons Company
    Headquarters Company
    Weapons Company
    Rifle Companies
        "I" Company (India)
        "K" Company (Kilo)
        "L" Company (Lima)
        "M" Company (Mike) (This was my company.)
Mike Company consisted of Three Platoons (One officer designated as Platoon Commander)
        1st Platoon
        2nd Platoon
        3rd Platoon (This was my platoon.)
3rd **Platoon** consisted of Three Squads (One man designated as Squad Leader)

1st Squad

2nd Squad

3rd Squad (This was my squad when I first arrived.)
3rd Squad consisted of Three Fire Teams (4-man teams, one man designated as Fire Team Leader)
1st Fire Team, 2nd Fire Team, 3rd Fire Team

- When I first arrived, I was assigned as a Rifleman in the 1st Fire Team, 3rd Squad, 3rd Platoon of Mike Company.
- The Battalion Weapons Company would usually assign 1 or 2, 60-caliber machine gun teams to each platoon. A machine gun team consisted of 1- gunner and 1 loader/ammo carrier.

Chapter 1 Notes:

Colfax Women's Club Park
This park was built on a hill and terraced. Besides serving as a location for musical shows and productions, a favorite activity, in these simpler times, was rolling all the way down the hill, leaving one dizzy, disoriented, and giggling uncontrollably at the bottom.

Colfax Library
Is a Carnegie library, built with money donated by Scottish-American businessman and philanthropist Andrew Carnegie. A total of 2,509 Carnegie libraries were built between 1883 and 1929, including some belonging to public and university library systems.

Chapter 2 Notes:

Marine infantry and artillery battalions are commonly designated by a battalion number-slash- regiment number. So the 3rd Battalion of the 26th Marine Regiment was simply designated, "3/26".

Chapter 3 Notes:

Recon (Reconnaissance): There are 2 levels of Marine Recon training and assignments.

Battalion Recon is a part of a reinforce infantry battalion usually as part of the MAGTF (Marine Air Ground Task Force). They operate closer to friendly lines. Very similar in capability to Force Recon, but they usually do not insert using parachute. Their Recon missions are categorized as Division Level.

Force Recon generally operates independently and deeper behind enemy lines. During Vietnam, they utilized two mission types "Key Hole" and "Sting Ray." "Key Hole" was watch and don't get seen. "Sting Ray" was completely opposite, being more direct action.

Chapter 5 Notes:

Danang is one of the major port cities in Vietnam and the biggest city in Central Vietnam. The city is situated on the coast of the Eastern Sea, at the opening end of the Hàn River.

Some have argued that the Vietnamese War began at Danang. The US Marines were essentially the first dedicated US combat troops to be deployed in Vietnam; put ashore in the amphibious landings of the 9th Marine Expeditionary Brigade at Danang (March 8, 1965)[91].

Camp Evans was established by the 3rd Battalion 4th Marines[92] in late 1966 as part of Operation Chinook. The camp was located to the west of Highway 1, approximately 24 km northwest of Huế in Thừa Thiên–Huế Province. The camp was named after Marine Lance Corporal Paul Evans, who was the first Marine killed from our battalion during Operation Chinook.

---

[91] Pg. 81, "The Illustrated History of the Vietnam War" Andrew Wiest and Chris McNab.. Amber Books(2015)

[92] When 3rd Battalion, 26th Marines first landed in Vietnam, they were temporarily assigned to the 4th Marine Regiment while they built and occupied Camp Evans.

Of course Khe Sahn later became famous for the 71-day siege the troops endured there in ** and ** of 1968. It was subjected to heavy artillery and rocket fire, but the NVA was never able to break the siege. The 3/26 received its ** citation for its efforts in attacking the entrenched NVA forces in the hills around the base during the siege. This was after the fighting near Con Thien, so I was gone by then.

Chapter 7 Notes:

Ontos vehicles were originally developed by the Army, but the Army dropped the design. The Marines found them perfect for taking out groups of charging bad guys. One unique feature was that once all of the 106 mm recoilless rifles were shot, a crewman had to exit the Ontos to reload them.

Chapter 10 Notes:

The American Legion Post in Colfax, Iowa. Colfax Post 192, District # 7 of the American Legion received its charter on November 30th, 1920, approximately 15 months after the Congressional Charter for the American Legion was approved. Post 192 is a "Dough Boy" Post.

The building itself was a large, two-story building on the edge of town, just across the Skunk River from the Monroe Folding Table Company. The building may originally have been utilized as a plant for processing chickens (not sure). When the Legion Post took residence there, there was an attached bar and a large dance floor upstairs. In later years, the American Legion would hold "Steak Nights", once a month, serving some of the best steaks Iowa had to offer and followed up by an adult dance upstairs. When they were popular, there were also square dances held there as well.

Bibliography

"Memories of an Old Marine", Calvin Rhett Holley, Boggy Bottom Publishing Company

"Ambush Valley - I Corps, Vietnam 1967", Eric Hammel, Presidio Publishing Company

"Lima-6, A Marine Company Commander in Vietnam", Colonel Dick Campbell, Pacifica Press

"A Hellish Place of Angels, Con Thien", Daryl J. Eigen, iUniverse Books

"Uprooted: A Vietnamese Family's Journey, 1935-1975", David Lucas,

"Inside the VC and the NVA", Michael Lanning and Dan Cragg, Ballantine Books

"Vietnam 1967-68: U.S. Marine vs. NVA Soldier", David R. Higgins, Osprey Publishing

"To Hear Silence, Charlie battery, 1st Battalion, 13th Marines", Ronald Hoffman, On Demand Publishing

"The Hill Fights, The First Battle of Khe Sanh", Edward Murphy, Ballantine Books

Glossary of Terms and Acronyms

Actual: The [Marine] unit commander. Used to distinguish the commander from the radioman when the call sign is used.

AK-47: Soviet-manufactured Kalashnikov semi-automatic and fully automatic combat assault rifle, fires a 7.62-mm at 600 rounds per minute; the basic weapon of the NVA It has a distinctive popping sound.

AO: Area of Operations.

Arc Light: Code name for B-52 bombers strikes along the Cambodian-Vietnamese border. These operations shook earth for ten miles away from the target area.

ARVN: Army of The Republic of Vietnam

bandoliers: Ammo belts for rifles and machine guns.

base camp: A resupply base for field units and a location for headquarters of brigade or division size units, artillery batteries and air fields. Also known as the "rear area."

battery: A artillery unit equivalent to a company. Six105mm or 155mm howitzers or two 8-inch or 175mm self-propelled howitzers.

bird dog: Light observation plane. Used to identify and mark targets for air support. Often came under ground fire from enemy troops.

blood trail: A trail of blood left by a fleeing man who has been wounded.

body count: The number of enemy killed, wounded, or captured during an operation.

Bouncing Betty: Antipersonnel mine with two charges: the first propels the explosive charge upward, and the other is set to explode at about waist level.

bush: Infantry term for the areas outside of a base perimeter that were either jungle or heavily foliaged areas.

C-4: Plastic, putty textured explosive carried by infantry soldiers. It burns when lit and would boil water in seconds instead on minutes, used to heat C-rations in the field and to blow up bunkers.

C-130: Large, propeller-driven, Air Force planes that carry people and cargo; the Hercules.

CH-54: Largest of the American helicopters, strictly for cargo. Also called Flying Crane or Skycrane.

Cache: Hidden supplies.

Casualty: This will usually refer to someone who has been KIA (Killed In Action), or WIA (Wounded In Action), or otherwise incapacitated to the point where they can no longer effectively fight. A good example of this is when a unit has "heat casualties"; individuals who have succumbed to heat stroke. Heat stroke can be very serious and even deadly.

Charlie: Viet Cong or NVA.

Chicom: Chinese communist made weapons or gear. Example, Chicom grenade."

Claymore: A antipersonnel mine, that when detonated, propels small, steel projectiles in a 60-degree fan-shaped pattern, to a maximum distance of 100 meters. Used by Allied infantrymen.

Concertina wire: Coiled barbed wire with razor type ends

contact: Firing on or being fired upon by the enemy.

C-rations: Combat rations. Canned meals for use in the field. Each usually consisted of a can of some basic course, a can of fruit, a packet of some type of dessert, a packet of powdered coca, sugar, powder cream, coffee, a small pack of cigarettes, two pieces of chewing gum, and toilet paper.

Det-cord: Detonating cord, used with (or as) explosives. Different than "time fuse." which usually burns a 3 feet per second. Det-cord burns at 26,000 feet per second, which basically makes it an explosive device. It is used when explosives like C-4 are not adequate due to the shape of the object. Example, to blow up a tree, wrap the Det-cord around the circumference of the tree several times. Attach a 2 foot time fuse, then light the time fuse and you have several minutes to get to a safe distance. When the time fuse reaches the Det-cord, it starts to burn rapidly (26,000 ft. per sec.), and the tree is blown neatly in half.

DMZ: Demilitarized zone. The dividing line between North and South Vietnam established in 1954 at the Geneva Convention.
Doc: Medic or corpsman. A deferential term that Marines use to address their corpsmen. A Navy corpsman travels with all Marine platoons out in the field, and are historically held in very high esteem by all combat Marines.

E-tool: Entrenching tool. Folding shovel carried by infantrymen.

FAC: Forward Air Control.
Fast Mover: Any jet aircraft.
Fixed Wing: Any aircraft, which is not a helicopter.
FO: See Forward Observer.
Fire base: Temporary or semi-permanent artillery encampment used for fire support of forward ground operations
Firefight: A battle, or exchange of small arms fire with the enemy.
Forward observer. A person attached to a field unit to coordinate the placement of direct or indirect fire from ground, air, and naval forces.

Free fire zone: Free to fire upon any forces you may come upon…Do not have to identify. Sometimes called free kill zones. Everyone is deemed hostile, and a legitimate target.

Friendly fire: Accidental attacks on U.S. or allied soldiers by other U.S. or allied soldiers.

G-2: The short answer is, that G-2 refers to the Intelligence Section. The "G" stands for "General" staff. The 2 designates the unit's intelligence office. So G-2 is the intelligence office for a headquarters commanded by a General. (Division, Corp, etc.) S-2 is the intelligence office for a headquarters commanded by a Colonel (Battalion level). There are other staff offices as well. S-1, personnel; S-2, intelligence; S-3, Operations; S-4, Supply, etc.

Grids: Map broken into numbered thousand-meter squares.

Grunt: Infantryman.

HE: High explosive artillery round.

Heat tabs: Flammable tablet used to heat C-rations. Can take a long time to heat the food and gave off harsh fumes. Some infantrymen would carry around chuck of C-4 and then chisel off a small piece to heat their food or coffee in a very short period of time.

Hooch: Living quarters.

Hot LZ: A landing zone under enemy fire.

H&S Company: Headquarters & Service Company, which contains the Command Staff and the S-1,2,3 & 4 sections mentioned in the reference to "G-2."

Huey: Light attack and transport helicopter.

I Corps: The northernmost military region in South Vietnam. There were 4 military regions dividing up South Vietnam (I, II, III, IV). Region I was pronounced as "Eye Corps").

II Corps: The Central Highlands military region in South Vietnam

III Corps: The densely populated, fertile military region between Saigon and the Highlands

IV Corps: The marshy Mekong Delta, southernmost military region.

Immersion foot: A condition resulting from feet being submerged in water for a prolonged period of time, causing cracking and bleeding.

In-country: Being physically in Vietnam.

K-bar: Combat knife, used by Marines.

KIA: Killed in action.

Kit Carson scout: Former Viet Cong who act as guides for U.S. military units.

Klick: 1 Kilometer, or 1000 meters.

L: A type of ambush set-up, shaped like the letter 'L'.

LAW: Light Anti-Tank Weapon. A shoulder-fired, 66-millimeter rocket. The launcher tube is made of fiberglass. It telescopes out to its full length when preparing to fire, and is disposable after one shot.

LP: A Listening Post is usually a two man* position, set up at night outside the perimeter away from the ....main body of troopers, which acted as an early warning system against attack. *In US Army, these are usually four man teams.

LRRP: Long Range Reconnaissance Patrol. An elite team, usually composed of five to seven men who go deep into the jungle to observe enemy activity without initiating contact.

LT: Lieutenant.

Lurps: Members of Long Range Reconnaissance Patrols, also can refer to dehydrated food package replacing c-rations.

LZ: Landing zone. Usually, a small clearing secured temporarily for the landing of resupply helicopters or to pick up troops, via helicopter.

M-14: A 7.62mm caliber rifle that fired semi and full automatic. Used in early portion of Vietnam conflict. The Marine Corps transitioned over to the M-16 in March of 1967.

M-16: The standard U.S. military rifle used in Vietnam from 1966 on. Successor to the M-14. The M-16 utilized ammunition of a 5.56 caliber, which was smaller, and lighter. Note: The Army transitioned to the M-16 first, the Marines Corps transitioned in March of 1967.

M-60: The standard, lightweight machine gun used by U.S. forces in Vietnam.

M-79: A U.S. military hand-held grenade launcher. The round (or grenade) was shaped like a very large rifle round, and would spin as it exited the launcher tube. The round would not arm itself until the round had completed a certain number of rotations, i.e., distance. Because of its distinctive report, it has earned the nicknames of "Thumper." "Thump-Gun." "Bloop Tube." and "Blooper" among American soldiers; Australian units referred to it as the "Wombat Gun." [93]

---

[93] I was walking in a column once, and the grenadier in front of me accidently discharged his M-79. The round was propelled out the tube and struck the helmet of the Marine walking in front of him, and then glanced off and landed somewhere in the bushes. The grenade did not detonate, although the Marine was knocked cold and had a large dent in his helmet. The round had not rotated enough times to arm the grenade.

Marker round: The first round fired by mortars or artillery. Used to adjust the following rounds onto the target.

Medevac: Medical evacuation from the field by helicopter.

MIA: Missing In Action.

Minigun: A Rapid fire machine gun with multi-barrels that is electronically controlled, capable of firing up to 6,000 rounds a minute, primarily used on choppers and some aircraft.

Montagnard: A French term for a number of tribes of mountain people inhabiting the hills and mountains of central and northern Vietnam. Vietnam was a former French Colony, and some of their phrases carried forth from the French Colonial days. The Montagnards were extremely loyal to the Army Special Forces units who sometimes trained them to fight alongside them. In addition, Marine units operating in the Central Highlands areas would employ them as scouts. Though ostracized and sometimes persecuted by both the South and the North Vietnamese governments, their loyalty and bravery became almost legendary within the Green Beret and Marine units that they operated with. Strong bonds remain even to this day.[94]

Mortar: Consisting of 3 parts; a steel tube, base plate, and tri-pod. A round is dropped in the tube, striking a firing pin, causing the projectile to leave the tube at a high angle. U.S. forces typically used 61mm and 80 mm mortars.

MOS: A number designating **a** Military Occupational Specialty. Example, a Marine rifleman has an MOS of 0311. A machine gunner would be 0331.

MP: Military police

MPC: Military payment currency. The scrip U.S. soldiers were paid in.

---

[94] [94] In the 1980's, Green Beret veterans of the Vietnam War set up foundations to help bring some of the Montagnards and their families to the U.S., and to also provide scholarships for young Montagnards who were still back there so they would be able to complete their educations. Much is left to do. (For more information about see the website "Save the Montagnard People".)

MSR: Main Supply Route.

mule: A small, motorized platform often used for transporting supplies and personnel.

napalm: A jellied petroleum substance which burns fiercely, used against enemy personnel.

NCO: Non-commissioned officers, usually obtain their position of authority by promotion through enlisted ranks. In contrast, commissioned officers hold higher ranks than NCOs, have more legal responsibilities, are paid more, and often have more non-military training such as a university diploma.

NVA: North Vietnamese Army.

OCS: Officer Candidate School.

POW: Prisoner of War.

PRC-25: Portable Radio Communications, Model 25. A back-packed FM receiver-transmitter used for short-distance communications. The range of the radio was 5-10 kilometers, depending on the weather, unless attached to a special, non-portable antenna which could extend the range to 20-30 kilometers. The radio itself was waterproof, but the handset was not, so care had to be taken when crossing streams.[95]

"Puff the Magic Dragon": An AC-47 (the military version of the DC-3 aircraft) that had been modified to provide devastating ground fire support using mini-guns that could deliver three second bursts of 7.62 rounds that would effectively cover half the area of a football field. They also dropped illumination flares.

Punji sticks: Sharpened bamboo sticks, usually covered with feces to poison the wound it inflicted.

QUAD-50s: A four-barrelled assembly of 50-caliber machine guns.

rack: Bed or cot.

---

[95] Sometimes, in the thick foliage and jungles of Vietnam, coverage could drop to much less than a kilometer at times.

R&R: Rest and Recreation. Two types: A three day, in-country, and a seven-day, out of county vacation. Grunts in the 8th Cav. Would receive a special R&R for the entire company. Usually after a major firefight. Marines would only get 1, seven-day, out of country vacation, once a year, usually after their first 6 months.

Rangers: Elite commandos and infantry, specially trained for reconnaissance and combat missions.

recon: Reconnaissance. Going out into the jungle to observe for the purpose of identifying enemy activity.

rotate: Returning to the U.S. after serving your tour in Vietnam

RPG: A rocket-propelled grenade. A Russian-made portable antitank grenade launcher.

ruck / rucksack: Backpack issued to infantry in Vietnam

saddle up: To put on one's pack and get ready to move out.

sapper: A Viet Cong or NVA solder who gets inside the perimeter, armed with explosives. Sappers went through rigorous special training.

satchel charges: A pack used by the enemy containing explosives that is dropped or thrown and is generally more powerful than a grenade.

Seabees: Navy construction engineers.

search and destroy: An operation in which Americans searched an area and destroyed anything which the enemy might find useful.

short-timer: A soldier nearing the end of his tour in Vietnam.

shrapnel: Pieces of metal, sent flying by an explosion.

smoke grenade: A grenade that released brightly colored smoke. Used for signaling choppers. Yellow was a safe LZ and Red was a hot LZ.

syrettes: A hypodermic needle connected to a collapsible tube. Contained morphine in most cases. After inserting the needle in the body, one would squeeze the morphine tube like toothpaste.

tracer: A round of ammunition chemically treated to glow so that its flight can be followed.

triage: The procedure for deciding the order in which to treat casualties.

trip flare: A ground flare triggered by a trip wire. Use to notify the approach of the enemy.

Trip wire: Typically, a wire or cord is attached to some explosive device.

UH-1H: A Huey helicopter.

VC: Viet Cong.

Victor Charlie: The Viet Cong; the enemy.

Vietnamization: U.S. policy, initiated by President Richard Nixon late in the war to turn over the fighting to the South Vietnamese Army during the phased withdrawal of American troops.

wake-up: The last day of a soldier's Vietnam tour. Example for 6 days: 5 days and a wake-up.

walking wounded: Wounded who are still able to walk without assistance.

wasted: killed

white phosphorus: an explosive round from artillery, mortars, or rockets, grenades. Also, a type of aerial bomb. When the rounds exploded, a huge puff of white smoke would appear from the burning phosphorus. When phosphorus hit the skin, it would continue to burn. Water would not put it out, it had to be smothered (mud might be used to seal off the wound) or it would continue to burn until it exited the body.

Willy Peter: White Phosphorus.

tree line: A row of trees at the edge of a field.

XO: Executive **Officer;** the second in command of a military unit.

zapped: Killed.

APPENDIX A

These were weapons I personally used or carried in Vietnam.

M-14 Rifle, 20-round magazine, 7.62mm rounds

M-6 bayonet for M14

M-16 Rifle, 20-round magazine, 5.56mm rounds

M-7 bayonet for M16

.45 Caliber Colt pistol

M26 and M61 grenades

Claymore mines

M72 LAW (Light Anti-Tank Weapon)

Yellow Smoke Grenade

C-4 Explosives

M-14 rifle: We carried the M-14 until mid-March of 1967 when they were replaced by the newer, lighter M-16 rifles. The M-14 used a 7.62 mm round and was preset in semi-automatic mode. The magazine would hold 20 rounds but we normally would load them with less to prevent any unexpected jamming.

M-16 rifle: We received our first M-16's in mid-March of '67. The very first thing we were required to do was to test fire them. The first rifles had several issues, the most egregious was that the powder in the shells was pushing the firing rate too high and they were susceptible to jamming a shell in the firing chamber. We would have to use cleaning rods, stored in the butt of the rifle to clear jams when residue would start to collect. To guard against a jam, we cleaned our rifles daily

.45 Colt pistol: I was not issued a pistol because I was always technically a rifleman. But because of my initial lack of confidence in the new M-16's, I acquired a pistol through the black market which I carried it in a shoulder holster beneath my flak jacket.

M-26 grenades: I always carried 2 or 3. The newer styles came with an additional safety featured called a "jungle pin." Basically, once the pin was pulled, a 2nd retaining clip had to be removed before it was armed. I never had access to anything except the original M-26's without the "jungle pins."

Claymore mines: We would sometimes be asked to carry extras of these by our squad leaders. They were usually used when setting up a defensive perimeter in the field.

M72 LAW: I only actually carried this twice in the field, and only once did I shoot it "in anger." and that time I fired high and missed with it.

Yellow smoke: Was usually used to mark a landing zone for helicopters and medevacs.

C-4: I would only carry small chunks of C-4, usually gotten from engineers. We would use those to boil water for coffee in a hurry.

Other Weapons Carried by Members of My Platoon

Lieutenant Manzi started out carrying a pump shotgun, in lieu of his M-16. Once we started getting into the denser jungle areas in the Central Highlands he would switch back to his M-16.

This is the **Remington 870, tactical shotgun** issued by the USMC early in the war; however, I think the lieutenant said that he was using a shotgun that had been sent from home that used to belong to either his father or grandfather.

The **M-79 grenade launcher**.

Sgt. Rhett Holley, loading his M-79 grenade launcher. The M79 grenade launcher is a single-shot, shoulder-fired, break-action grenade launcher that fires a 40x46mm grenade, which uses what the US Army calls the High-Low Propulsion System to keep recoil forces low. It first appeared during the Vietnam War. The M79 can fire a wide variety of 40 mm rounds, including explosive, anti-personnel, smoke, buckshot, flechette (pointed steel projectiles with a vaned tail for stable flight), and illumination.

The M60 is a belt-fed machine gun that fires the 7.62 mm NATO cartridge (.308 Winchester) commonly used in larger rifles. **It is generally used as a crew-served weapon and operated by a team of two or three individuals**. The team consists of the gunner, the assistant gunner (AG in military slang), and the ammunition bearer. The gun's weight and the amount of ammunition it can consume when fired make it difficult for a single soldier to carry and operate. The gunner carries the weapon and, depending on his strength and stamina, anywhere from 200 to 1000 rounds of ammunition. The assistant carries a spare barrel and extra ammunition, and reloads and spots targets for the gunner.

APPENDIX B

Some of the Most Common Weapons Carried by the Typical NVA Soldier

	AK-47 7.62mm ASSAULT RIFLE
	SIMONOV 7.62mm SELF-LOADING RIFLE (SKS)
	Chicom Type-56, 7.62mm ASSAULT RIFLE
	Type-24, 7.92mm HEAVY MACHINEGUN
	RPG-7 ROCKET LAUNCHER

APPENDIX C

Marine Rifle Company Structure

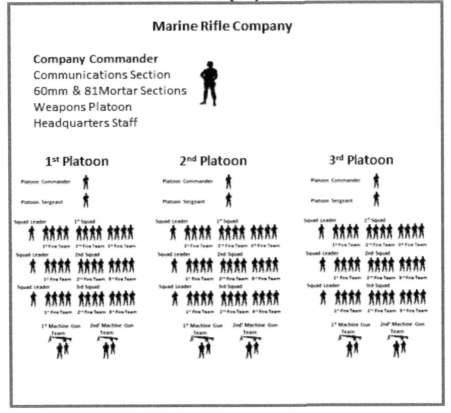

The official structure indicates that a standard platoon would have approximately 45 men, but it was more typical to have between 30-35 men when we went out into the field. Squad leaders would do double duty as a Fire Team leader, we might only have one man on each M-60 team, and there would be the inevitable people who were in sick bay, on R&R leave, or had been transferred out.

The standard Rifle Company, with the associated support sections, would typically be about 250-300 men, but when our company deployed out in the field, even taking our Weapons and Communication sections, we would more likely have only between 180 to 225 men at the most.

APPENDIX D

NVA Troop Structure

A typical NVA Battalion would have approximately 400–600 men, organized into 3 infantry companies and backed by a fire support (artillery, mortars, heavy machine guns) company. Recon, signals, sapper and logistics units rounded out the formation.

Each infantry company would have 3 platoons, as well as smaller elements of the fire support and logistic companies that come from their Battalion.

Below is a representation of a very basic NVA Platoon, but not showing the support elements who might be assigned to them.

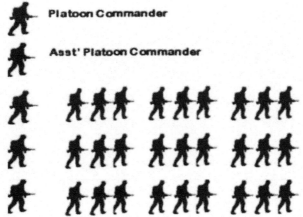

NVA Infantry Platoon

Platoon Commander

Asst' Platoon Commander

* NVA Infantry platoons rarely, if ever, carried radios.
* Communications was done through the use of runners.
* NVA Medics did not go into battle with infantry as did USMC Medics
• NVA Platoons were often augmented with additional men trained as snipers, sappers, or machine gun teams.

The End

Made in the USA
Columbia, SC
14 February 2023

11958047R00134